TRANSFORMATIONS
IN MODERN ARCHITECTURE

ARTHUR DREXLER

Front cover: John Portman & Associates. Renaissance Center, Detroit, Mich. 1971-77. Photo: Timothy Hursley/ Balthazar Korab Ltd.

Front flap: Langdon & Wilson, Architects. CNA Park Place, Los Angeles, Calif. 1968-71.

Inside front cover: Left: Manteola, Petchersky, Sanchez-Gomez, Santos, Solsona, Viñoly. Headquarters, Bank of the City of Buenos Aires, Argentina. 1968.

Right: Welton Becket Associates. Hyatt Regency Hotel and Reunion Tower, Dallas, Tex. 1973-78. Photo: Balthazar Korab

SECKER & WARBURG, LONDON

Acknowledgments

The exhibition on which this book is based took place at The Museum of Modern Art, New York, from February 23 through April 24, 1979. The exhibition was made possible through the generous support of The Graham Foundation for Advanced Studies in the Fine Arts and the PPG Industries Foundation.

I am especially grateful to the following individuals, who constituted an informal committee, for their assistance in collecting photographs and for their many helpful suggestions: Anna Querci, Milan; Brian Brace Taylor, Susan Day, Paris; Colin Amery, Lance Wright, London; and Shozo Baba, Yoshio Yoshida, Tokyo.

Special thanks must also be given to Mary Jane Lightbown for coordinating research and for assistance vital to the project; to Marie-Anne Evans for coping valiantly with manuscripts and correspondence; and to Jane Fluegel for invaluable editorial assistance.

A.D.

Contents

First published in England 1980 by Martin Secker & Warburg Limited, 54 Poland Street, London W1V 3DF.
Copyright © 1979 by The Museum of Modern Art, New York. All rights reserved. SBN 436 13711 9.
Designed by Patrick Cunningham, assisted by Keith Davis. Production by Timothy McDonough. Type set by M. J. Baumwell Typography, New York, N.Y. Printed by Eastern Press, Inc., New Haven, Conn. Bound by Sendor Bindery, New York, N.Y.
Printed in the United States of America.

Introduction

During the last two decades the history of modern architecture has been one of sorting out, developing, and transforming possibilities implicit at the beginning. What has changed more than architectural practice is the way we see buildings and talk about them. Underlying the change is the feeling, widespread but by no means universal, that the modern movement in architecture as understood by its pioneers is now over. That change in attitude describes a hope (or a fear) rather than a fact, and it also focuses attention on the nature of modernism.

It is unlikely that anyone can offer a definition of modern architecture to which there are no exceptions. But at the beginning of the modern movement one commitment emerged preeminent. Modern architecture, like engineering, sought to deal only with the truths of structure and function. It wanted all architectural pleasures to derive from the straightforward encounter with necessity. Architectural fictions, the play of unnecessary forms with which the historic styles sought to transcend necessity, were rejected as unworthy. That at least describes an essential characteristic of what came to be called the International Style, to which the most important exception was Expressionism in its various national modes—the loser, for a time, in the wars of persuasion.

But an architecture based on objective analysis alone is impossible —emotionally, logically, and even technically. Modern architecture has thus had a history of trying to escape from the internal contradictions of its own philosophy. Its forms have had to be justified according to determinist doctrines which the forms themselves contradict. For the most part those forms have remained within the reductionist parameters of engineering and technology, modified from year to year by developments in modern painting and sculpture, by the accelerated international publication of projects and built work, and by a quantity of building activity around the world without precedent in human history.

These factors have helped to bring about an altered perception of the social significance of architecture itself. Theories about housing and urban planning, for example, already suspect by 1960, and once held to be the very heart of modernism's special claim to ethical competence, by the end of the seventies have been largely repudiated for contributing to the environmental dysfunctions they were supposed to end. The arbitrary nature of certain forms and configurations, almost always derived from abstract sculpture, becomes more apparent as belief in their magical efficacy falters. Nor is the loss of confidence limited to dealing with large questions affecting the social order. It extends to each morning's decisions.

For the pioneers of the modern movement the "how" of building answered the "what." But by the end of the fifties what to build and how to build had again become two separate questions. Contradictory approaches were justified in the cause of variety—or in the higher cause of finding for each problem a uniquely appropriate solution. Soon the variety became, as Peter Collins has described it, "archaeologically unclassifiable," while the public (and a great many

3

architects) continued to feel that modern architecture was peculiarly monotonous. Thus in 1960, some months before his seventy-fifth birthday, when Ludwig Mies van der Rohe was asked to describe his working day he answered: "I get up. I sit on the bed. I think 'what the hell went wrong? We showed them what to do'".

Mario Pani Architect & Associates. Ciudad Tlatelolco Housing Project, Mexico City, Mexico. 1960-74

Opinions about what architecture ought to be have changed, during the last 20 years, against the background of traumatic public events. Many of these events, worldwide in their impact, have had their locus in the United States. Americans have experienced three political assassinations; an unpopular war, which was lost; economic instability; a reduction in the supply of energy before it had been expected; and a growing fear that technology has become unmanageable. In the midst of these harrowing experiences are some technological triumphs: sending the first men to the moon must be a decisive event, even if other events have made it seem almost a minor footnote to what really concerns us.

As many observers have noted, there are now more architects practicing their profession than ever before, and the number of students in training exceeds both the number of architects and the capacity of even the most productive and well-regulated society to employ them. Inevitably, many of these students will never practice architecture. But their training is bound to affect their judgment when they become clients, and it has already affected their role as an audience. An appetite for the imagery of architecture improves self-confidence in telling architects how to do their work, or in doing it for them.

The study of architecture seems to be replacing the study of law as a respectable and benevolent pursuit. But unlike law it cannot be contained within rigorously defined standards of professionalism: in the United States the tendency to eliminate professional certification of architects is strong enough to provoke opposition from the American Institute of Architects.

Critical discourse has shifted away from the profession. The most instructive commentary no longer comes from practicing architects who incidentally teach, and whose comments are interesting because their work commands admiration, but rather from academics who may or may not be architects, or architects who build, and for whom critical discourse is regulated by its own laws of production and distribution. Within this network, the connoisseur's cultivation of sensibility yields to what might be called technical gossip; aesthetics is seen as philosophy, and philosophy is seen as an examination of the structure of meaning, but not necessarily of what is meant.

Whatever it is that architecture is supposed to mean, the words used for praise or condemnation have largely changed their roles. "Functional" perhaps meant nothing in particular to begin with, but was often useful in persuading clients that modernism's bare utilitarian style could be efficient and cheap. Today "functional" has no place in serious discourse about the nature of architecture, either as praise or blame, but "un-functional" may still be used in the old philistine way to disparage the pursuit of aesthetics.

Sune Lindström, Olle Elgquist, HSB Construction Department. Grintorp Apartment Buildings, Taby, Sweden. 1957-66

Emile Aillaud. Housing, Pantin-les-Courtillieres, France. 1954-59

"Clean," "simple," "pure," "elegant," all once used to suggest the virtues of austerity, have been devalued into something rather different. Their unsuccessful modes, once laughable, are now admired. "Simple" is now "slick." To be fussy, busy, and vulgar is proof of a knowing disdain for simplicity—which is now seen to be inimical to the natural fullness of life. "Complexity" is put forward as a goal more in keeping with reality—and, it may be said, the tendency toward complexity is not without poetic justice.

"Strong," "tough," and "brutal" are post–World War II terms of praise (although used earlier by the Futurists to evoke the joy of industrial dynamism and warfare), and often serve as euphemisms for "monumental," a word which may not yet be used without nervous apprehension. But "strong," "tough," and "brutal" describe qualities presently less gratifying than those now designated by "crazy," "wild," and "camp." The parody tends to become the norm.

"Abstract" remains a more or less constant value for that part of modern architecture still under the spell of abstract painting and sculpture. "Contextual," implying a due regard for what is happening around you, is a term of praise difficult to reconcile with a taste for the abstract, although the effort is often made.

"Taste" itself is conceivable only contextually—that is, it enters sophisticated discourse for purposes of comparison. What was called "bad taste" in the forties is now seen to be ripe with "meaning." Those who actually have bad taste think they have its opposite, but "good taste" is a quality or condition no serious architect would now claim for his own work, lest it be misunderstood as representing "middle-class values," which middle-class intellectuals disdain.

The odor of "good taste" can often be dispelled by the introduction of "meaning," as long as meaning is retrieved from formerly unacceptable sources (the archaic, the moderne and streamlined, and the more domestic forms of the inept). But as the demand for meaning increases, new—or old—sources of supply must be found. This has helped to change the import of "historicizing," formerly inadmissible but now a new frontier of meaning. Like historicizing, "eclecticism" is the beneficiary of a separate and in this case prior rehabilitation. It is the aesthetic counterpart of "pluralism," which is now understood as a socially desirable and positive form of tolerance. But tolerance is a dangerous word because it implies a dominant position from which lesser manifestations may be patronized. Thus the new pluralism will encounter its defeat, when the time comes for reintegration, under the tutelage of a single intolerant purpose. Meanwhile the accumulating examples of coherent alternate views may yet rehabilitate the word "style."

A peculiarity of "meaning" would seem to be that it cannot be found in the immediate present. It can be found in the past, even the recent past of modernism's minor modes, or in the future, as in the varieties of science-fiction decor characterized by Colin Rowe as "Futurist Revival," but the present as such is increasingly "meaningless." There are, however, at least two important exceptions: Las Vegas has been cited as a part of the present that is rich with meaning: we can learn from it how to design for compulsive behavior.

Disneyland is considered less rewarding, even though so much of it deals quite cleverly with the past, but that may be because the inane is less interesting than the vicious.

Rapid shifts in value, and perhaps cynicism, make it difficult for some observers to take competing views of architecture altogether seriously. Reversals of judgment are seldom complete and never without ulterior motives. What was bad, for quite specific reasons, is declared good for the same reasons. Treason, Talleyrand remarked, is a matter of dates.

More than any other historic style modern architecture has been dependent on manifestos, theoretical projects, and publicity. Without reference to its programs of education, and the avowed or implicit aim of social revolution with which it began and with which many of its theorists are still concerned, its architectural intentions are not always fully explained. Architects know that certain buildings, whatever their merits as usable architecture, are really to be appreciated as allusions to certain projects, unbuilt or unbuildable, which constitute a second order of architectural history. We have had a built architecture which tends to justify itself by citing what it has not been able to build.

Abundant opportunities to build in the sixties, despite faltering convictions, perhaps helped to deflect purely theoretical studies toward social criticism cast as architectural jokes. We live overwhelmed by machines: therefore why not walking machine-cities on mechanical legs, of science-fiction comic-strip provenance, as in the entertaining drawings of the English group Archigram? And existential nausea ought to have its architectural mode, so why not the surreal perspectives of "utility grids" covering the earth, as in the Antonioniesque productions of the Italian group Superstudio? Deliberately ambiguous, these and similar studies—especially those accompanied by left-wing political expectations—owe much of their charm to uncertainty. Since they cannot be serious they must be jokes, unless they are meant to be warnings.

Alienation is often held to be the condition natural to our time, but it has never been clear why architects should make the condition more pervasive, except as a tactic of subversion for political ends. For that purpose such projects might best be evaluated for their chances, if built, of provoking revolution. Insofar as the spirit of subversion pervades some built works, the result would seem to be that they postpone revolution by increasing the tolerance for alienation.

Of course during the last 20 years there have been important projects, and commissioned buildings that have remained only projects, that do not have social criticism as their primary justification. Some are of interest because they push a technology slightly beyond its normal application; others are of interest because they explore ideas that are only just beginning to find clients. For the sixties it is the projects of the twenties that best explain architectural intentions. In the seventies perhaps the most significant projects deal with the incorporation of historical forms, and the rapid acceptance of such ideas by corporate as well as private clients renders them

WED Enterprises, Inc. Disney World, Lake Buena Vista, Fla. 1965–71

less instructive as projects than as built work. In any case, the public is left with what has been built—actual buildings—for which theory or the promise of revolution is not always adequate consolation.

Judgment is hampered not only by the overwhelming volume of theory, but by the sheer quantity of published work—and what is published represents only a fraction of what is built each year. Information about buildings depends on surrogate materials—photographs, models, drawings—and the manner in which images are selected and organized is central to the selection of buildings for this book, as it was for the exhibition that preceded it.

Mass journalism for the general public oscillates between the unique and the average, but its choices are most often governed by the potential for "controversy." The merely good, which may not be in dispute, is least eligible for public scrutiny; it is difficult to imagine a newspaper article that says: here are some good buildings—none of them has won a prize and they are in no way peculiar.

Professional journals whose primary purpose is to document what seems to be the best work must make their selections within the limits imposed by a fixed number of pages. Extensive presentation of one building necessarily crowds out many others; the equal documentation of many buildings tends to subordinate them as members of a class. Most often it is a class defined by use or by a set of technical problems: here are 10 houses, or 10 hotels, or 20 prefabricated schools. Within each class, the greater the variations the more interesting and useful such surveys are felt to be.

But it is most unlikely that a selection of buildings would be made on the basis of comparable aesthetics: here are 10 minimal sculptures designed for a variety of uses. Classification by aesthetic intent emphasizes choices freely made by the architect. Since even the happiest of these free choices will seldom be acknowledged as such by the architects who made them, and since they are sometimes difficult to explain, it is easier to talk about something else. Most criticism does talk about something else, broadening the external references but narrowing the choice of examples. Increasing the examples but narrowing the discussion to aesthetic intent, as much as possible, has the advantage of dealing more directly with what architects choose to do because they think it is beautiful.

Museum exhibitions of architecture have conflicting purposes. In the thirties they presented a new architecture that the public could see nowhere else and that architects could not see as much of even in the professional journals. Such exhibitions drew on some 20 years of work, much of it the primary statement of the new architectural aesthetic, much of it interesting diversification of its possibilities.

By the early fifties this aesthetic had begun to gain government and business patronage, particularly in the United States. Exhibitions could call attention to these expanding opportunities, illustrating in detail work that was believed to be excellent while assuring patrons and public alike that its proliferation was desirable. Validation of the best of the new (with occasional reappraisals of the old as proto-new) was believed to serve the interests of both lay and professional audiences.

In the seventies the interests of those audiences have diverged. Validation is beside the point: no one needs to be persuaded that the new is good when the appetite for something new exceeds the capacity to produce it. Nor is architectural reportage appropriate or even practical, given the nature of a museum. Architects, in any case, keep up with the new through professional journals rather than relatively infrequent exhibitions, and the same is true for a public well served by architectural reporting in newspapers and popular magazines.

Therefore it is not surprising that a professional audience might more than ever expect an exhibition to declare that *this* work is excellent and worthy of comparison with the great work of the past, at the same time implying that all other comparable work may be ignored. It is an expectation best met by reducing, rather than increasing, the work under review. The profession responds to exclusivity.

The public, on the other hand, although it may share the professional's interest in annual nominations to a Hall of Fame, has a certain interest in the generality of architectural practice—as indeed the majority of architects, whose talents and opportunities may preclude stardom, must also have. The habit of reduction to the "best" examples distorts the issues and forestalls certain kinds of judgments.

Underlying distinctions between the uniquely excellent, the ordinarily good, and the acceptable average is a difference between architecture and the other arts. Modern architecture claims to be able to make the world both physically and psychologically better to live in. Its avowed aim is to transform the real world. It has attempted to do this by translating the uniquely excellent into general practice.

When general practice suffers from the translation, it is no service to the cause of excellence to insist that general practice has failed. It is more logical to reexamine the ideas that have been held superior in the light of what happens to them when they are broadly applied—unless one is willing to abandon the idea that the art of architecture must have broad application. That might be a fair choice, but it is not the choice that modern architecture made in its formative years, nor has the commitment to universal applicability ever been renounced. Indeed, the modern movement has been distinguished by the well-intentioned but reckless belief that its principles can and must deal with every conceivable problem.

With all of the foregoing in mind, it is reasonable to suppose that there will have been produced during the last 20 years not 10 or 50 but 400 or even 4,000 buildings that illuminate the exchange of architectural ideas through their primary statement, their adaptation to normative use, their hold on our sensibilities, and their rapid devaluation. It is also reasonable to expect that among 400 buildings will be most of the major achievements of the period.

In an exhibition variations on a theme can be presented almost simultaneously, the number of direct comparisons being limited chiefly by the 10 or 12 images the eye can take in at once—but expanded by the perspectives possible in a gallery. In a book the number of direct comparisons is limited to the images that can be accommodated on facing pages. Such comparisons may then acquire exaggerated significance. Verbal explanation must intrude, to some degree lessening the force of visual evidence. Thus the groupings feasible in the exhibition, although here substantially retained, have been reduced in quantity and occasionally modified. The result nevertheless includes 362 of the exhibition's 406 images.

The criteria of selection have not necessarily applied to a building in its totality. Photographs have been chosen because they seem to capture the essential idea, whether in whole or in part, and most of the selections conform to those approved by the architects. Plans and sections have been omitted because they do not contribute directly to the impressions an observer receives when passing by an actual building (although it must be admitted that some modern buildings require the posting of plans for anyone intending to go inside).

The conjoining of different kinds and degrees of quality is problematic. Despite arguments to the contrary, some architects will feel that true excellence is denigrated when made to share a spotlight with work that may resemble it only superficially. That may remain a question of individual judgment; more important is that narrowing the comparisons to similarities in aesthetic choice focuses attention on the borrowing of formal ideas customary to architecture. This raises questions of priority, which is to say of originality.

We would not judge the quality of a painting by Picasso according to the quality of its imitations. No one studying painting is taught to paint Picassos, nor are imitation Picassos highly regarded. But architectural ideas are models. Part of their value is that they *can* be imitated, varied, "improved." No matter how strongly the modern movement stressed the idea of approaching each problem without prior commitments—as if the wheel had to be perpetually reinvented—any successful solution to an architectural problem embodies a previous success, and is itself successful in that it can be imitated.

Yet skill in imitation is seldom advertised as a matter of merit. On the contrary, the more dependent a work may be on received ideas, the more passionately emphasized are its slightest innovations or refinements. Now that imitation is not as focused on the work of three or four great, pioneering figures, the movement of ideas is less from father to son and more from brother to brother. Competition and the ambivalence architects feel about originality make it awkward to discuss an individual's use of a shared idea—but not necessarily the limitations of the idea itself.

The effects buildings produce are primarily and unavoidably visual. Evaluation might therefore benefit by setting aside the program notes, the manifestos, the moral injunctions with which architecture is so often launched on a helpless world. Buildings are designed by individuals, or groups of individuals, who must function as artists and who have personal predispositions towards certain kinds of form.

An architect whose greatest pleasure is to shape intricate sculptures will strive to do so no matter how inopportune a particular occasion may be. An architect whose happiness it is to solve problems—connecting one piece of structure to another, for example—will tend to avoid the outright production of sculpture. For some architects neither solving problems nor making sculptures will suffice: their abiding interest is a mise-en-scène that embraces much more than their own work. In a way their diffidence is ultimately more demanding, in that it stakes out a larger claim.

The thing in itself, independent of technique; technique in itself, independent of the thing it makes; the thing and the technique in the service of what already exists—few architects are wholly given to just one kind of response. Different intentions may combine to produce in one work a result admired for integrating disparate possibilities—and the same work may be rejected because it is not "pure." During the last 20 years attitudes toward pure versions of anything have changed, but the architecture of the period may still be usefully examined within these broad groupings:

Post-World War II interpretations of Cubism and Expressionism, in which architecture is seen primarily as the invention of sculptural form;

Structural design, in which architecture is seen as the systematic solution of technical problems;

Regional or vernacular building, in which the forms of modern architecture are subordinated to traditional modes.

Prior to World War II, modern architecture was largely concerned with planar effects of volume and transparency. Using smooth surfaces of white stucco and large areas of glass, it created an image characteristically light, airy, and cheerful. But by the early thirties this idiom was already felt to be too limited. Its range was broadened by the introduction of natural materials, like the stone wall in Le Corbusier's Pavillon Suisse, and by effects of rusticity contrasted with the elegance of new, technically refined materials.

By 1946 the balance had changed. Le Corbusier's postwar work, particularly the Marseilles apartment house, the Jaoul houses, and the chapel at Ronchamp, led the way toward a new preoccupation with mass, weight, rough textures, and deliberately crude workmanship. Where light and transparency had once been associated with physical and mental health, the new ponderousness was accompanied by no formal justification but was understood to be of an emotional resonance in keeping with the "age of anxiety."

In Europe and England the style recalled wartime German fortifications like those on the English Channel, and often echoed the bizarre contrasts of scale produced by such sinister apparitions as Friedrich Tamms' antiaircraft towers in Vienna. This style was applied with equal enthusiasm to museums, theaters, housing, schools—to virtually everything except factories, which continued to be built in less cumbersome ways.

Brutalism, as the style has been called, is aggressive form not necessarily dependent on exposed concrete (Le Corbusier's *béton brut).* Its spirit has influenced the use of other materials in less dynamic ways of building. American versions are relatively calm and tend to the impersonal smoothness of "minimal" or "primary form" sculpture,

LeCorbusier. Unité d'Habitation, Marseilles, France. 1946–52

Le Corbusier. Jaoul Houses, Neuilly, France. 1954–56

Le Corbusier. Chapel of Notre Dame du Haut, Ronchamp, France. 1950-54

German fortifications, Longy Common, Alderney, Channel Islands. WW II

Friedrich Tamms. Antiaircraft fortification, Vienna, Austria. WW II

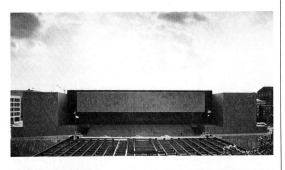

Victor Lundy. United States Tax Court (two views), Washington, D.C. 1967-74

which they resemble and which they may have influenced. Smooth or rough, the message is essentially the same. "Brutal" describes not so much a single mode of architectural composition as a taste for the intimidating, the gratuitously hostile.

Other sculptural modes less indebted to Cubism have persisted, and however violent their effects they are seldom perceived as Brutalist. The angular, faceted, and largely opaque masses used by Gottfried Böhm in his extraordinary churches are exemplary of latter-day Expressionism. Most building programs cannot be made to sustain such fiercely introspective moods, and not surprisingly there are only a few persuasive examples cast as apartment houses or concert halls. But in another sense all Brutalist architecture is a mode of Expressionism, in that its forms "express" an emotional content independent of the "objective" facts of structure and function.

Occasionally the expressive content of a building that is conceived as a minimalist sculpture, like Victor Lundy's in Washington, D.C., bears some plausible relationship to its program. Thus, the blank, formal symmetry and the threatening mass cantilevered 55 feet seem appropriate enough when one learns that the building is the United States Tax Court.

A second alternative to Cubism is the curvilinear style in which buildings resemble the forms of living organisms rather than hard-edged geometric masses. Most architects predisposed to this literal version of organic form have sought maximum continuity of surface and space. This goal is incompatible with most planning requirements; and as might be expected, its pursuit is usually confined to houses. Nevertheless, the use of biologically organic form in architecture is a peculiarly modern development that has had a greater following in the postwar years than ever before. It is sustained by its own apparatus of theory and holistic philosophy. Concerned with the psychological effects of enclosure, its proponents have argued for a genuinely radical break with all forms of right-angled, cellular composition, which they see as inherently oppressive.

Structuralist design in its purest form deals with what Mies van der Rohe called "skin and bones" architecture: a steel or concrete skeleton structure covered by a glass or metal skin. Although Mies's own projects for glass skyscrapers in the twenties emphasized the skin and showed no structure at all, his American work increasingly concentrated on the bones until even the skin had its own external armature of metal mullions.

Some architects at the beginning of the sixties sought to abstract the skeletal cage still further by modifying its proportions and eliminating as much detail as possible. Others, perhaps in response to the work of sculptor-architects in various Brutalist modes, have sought to give to skeletal structure itself an expressive plastic complexity. Still others have borrowed the look of machinery or the bulky joints of a child's Tinker Toy. And a fascination with the possibilities of structure for its own sake sometimes leads to gymnastic exercises, hurling great blocks of buildings into the air for no reason more persuasive than that it can be done.

What these approaches have in common is their reliance on some aspect of structure to communicate interesting visual information about a building, other than the nature of its use. Paradoxically, the latest (perhaps the final) stage of this architecture returns to the earlier preeminence of the skin, for which metal and glass cladding systems have been so refined as to communicate almost nothing. Of all transformations of formal and technical ideas this one is perhaps the most striking, having now come full circle to take up again one of the enduring fantasies of the twenties.

Because the aesthetic impulse behind these technical developments minimizes visible detail, their origin in problems of structural design tends to be obscured. Having arrived at the perfect, infinitely extendable skin, there is little the problem-solving architect can do with it besides wrap it around an odd shape. Some architects have preferred eccentric parallelograms; others have preferred shapes derived from traditional masonry architecture. In either case the shapes, as they become noticeable in themselves, begin to confuse the issue. Perhaps the best of these skin-buildings are the least self-consciously designed: the plain supermarket packages in predictable shapes and sizes.

It is arguable that structuralists intent on solving problems succeed more often than sculptors intent on making expressive works of art. Sculpture requires a modicum of talent, which is imponderable; problem-solving requires aptitude. Successful sculpture is difficult to copy; successful problem-solving is cumulative and usually improves in the process. Nevertheless if the sculptor risks the outright hostility of the public, the problem-solver risks indifference. Indifference may soon become hostility, and when it does it is because of a pervasive sense that the wrong problems are being solved.

Modern architecture tends to develop by a process of exaggeration. If the structural elements of a particularly striking work are too thin or too fat, the first wave of imitations will make them thinner or fatter; the second wave will try to do the same with all remaining elements.

This process, perhaps unconscious, exerts a centrifugal force on coherent systems of design and ultimately reduces them to parodies. Attention then turns to the design of individual elements that can be elaborated without dependence on any single mode of architectural coherence. Windows, roofs, parapets—any element that can be isolated from a larger system can also be made to generate its own system.

Marginally related to these sometimes quite productive excursions is the use of painting at mural scale. In most cases abstract painting applied to architecture contributes little that would be missed if it were removed and installed in a gallery. In any case, it asks to be judged as painting. Only rarely has painting been made to contribute to architectural form in ways that significantly alter architectural intentions; even rarer is painting used to produce effects that would otherwise be impossible (see inside back cover).

When different kinds of form are combined in one building most observers make the assumption that the building is still meant to be perceived as a unified whole. If the forms are too unlike each other the

Alvar Aalto. Baker Dormitory (two views), M.I.T., Cambridge, Mass. 1947-48.

observer must work to keep track of their origins, mentally separating what the architect has combined or joining together what has been separated. In either case the perception of unity is usually thought to depend on the forms being to some degree compatible.

An important development during the last 20 years is the juxtaposition in one building of incompatible forms that cannot have evolved from one another, and are juxtaposed in order to insist on their unrelatedness. The result may fairly be called a hybrid, and the most disquieting examples appear to have been designed by opposing teams, recruited from sculptors and technicians, in a contest neither side wins (see page 100).

Hybrids of a sort can also be produced by contrasts within the same formal category. Alvar Aalto's Baker Dormitory for the Massachusetts Institute of Technology is an early (1947-48) and celebrated example. Its elevation facing the Charles River is a sinuous curve, ostensibly to give each room a view up or down the river. The curve stresses continuity and implies that the rear elevation must be simply the back of the same curve. But at the back the building is unexpectedly staccato, its angled planes tied together by a continuous stair climbing up the walls. The result is an unexpectedly "hybrid" configuration that challenges, but does not repudiate, the idea of unity.

Aalto's prewar architecture was only lightly tied to the orthodox International Style. It was admired rather more for its embodiment of regional (Scandinavian) qualities. In the Baker Dormitory, as in some buildings of the fifties, Aalto managed to synthesize a kind of one-man vernacular. Its flexibility is deceptive and less easily imitated than might be supposed, but some of Aalto's ideas have helped to sustain the legitimacy of a regional architecture disaffiliated from the International Style on principle.

"Regionalism" refers to an architecture of local characteristics—like Cape Cod cottages or Mexican patio houses—prompted by climate and available materials. Where it makes few or no references to classical styles it is usually called vernacular building, implying that it can be handled by craftsmen without an education in art history.

Regional or vernacular building is most often characterized by the use of a visible roof as a primary element of architectural composition; by a preference for natural materials used more or less as craftsmen have always used them; and by effects of small, almost domestic scale—even for fairly large public buildings.

Kinship with modernist abstraction was usually indicated, in the forties and fifties, by shed roofs rather than gables (sometimes as a compromise with zoning codes which forbade flat roofs); by the absence of decorative detail; and by a modest use of glass walls. The spontaneous ease of this kind of building influenced such European modernists transplanted to the United States as Marcel Breuer and Richard Neutra, both of whom gradually abandoned the white, planar abstraction of their first American houses for natural wood and pitched roofs. In principle such architecture was to have led to a normative style of wide applicability. In practice its opportunities were limited, until the fifties, to houses and other small-scale buildings outside the cities or in contexts essentially antiurban.

During the forties Regionalism was advocated, particularly in England and Scandinavia, as a more practical alternative to the theoretical rigors of the International Style, but at the same time it was dismissed as inadequate and sentimental. Since there is no such thing as regional glass or steel, the argument went, how could one justify regional architecture? And how could the regionalists ever cope with urban planning? But Regionalism did not fade away: it prospered. In town and country it has gradually extended its range to all kinds of buildings, even the skyscraper.

Associated with radical "alternate life style" movements as much as with political and cultural conservatism, Regionalism and its vernacular variations address problems of survival and coexistence —of historical continuity. By definition, Regionalism keeps the door open to historicizing, and historicizing cannot long be channeled within the limits of a single time or place. Its natural amplification is eclecticism.

One might expect that regional and vernacular building would by now be the subject of serious critical evaluation. Instead, it has been largely ignored even in those countries where its vitality is most obvious. Surveys of modern architecture in Japan, for example, pay scant attention to the continuing development of a tradition which used to be cited as one of the sources of Western modernism, and to which even today's modernist ideologues occasionally return for nourishment. In England, where the modern movement has incurred the most outspoken hostility, the available alternatives have not yet been the subject of sustained critical examination. This inability to come to grips with a substantial part of modern practice is all the more remarkable in that those historians who might have been expected to do so, by virtue of their sympathy for indigenous building, apparently respond to such work only when the cultures that produce it are poverty-stricken, archaic, or dead.

By the end of the seventies a self-conscious sort of picking at the past has begun to appear as a fresh possibility—intellectually respectable and perhaps even avant-garde. Yet historicizing work of the late fifties is still dismissed as frivolous, despite—or perhaps because of—its serious intent. Certain buildings of this kind may continue to seem inherently trivial. But many architects tried to deal with the problem of historical associations before criticism recognized its existence and the developments it implied. It was the reappearance of this problem during the fifties that clearly reflected the impoverishment of abstract, reductionist form.

Thus the United States Air Force Academy (1954-58), designed by Walter Netsch of Skidmore, Owings and Merrill, began as a demonstration of Miesian structural design and technical sophistication. Those characteristics were considered more appropriate to the client than allusions to a spurious history—although some members of Congress urged a Gothic-style Air Academy.

When the architect began to design a chapel within this group of buildings, the Miesian structural idiom in its most logical, reduc-

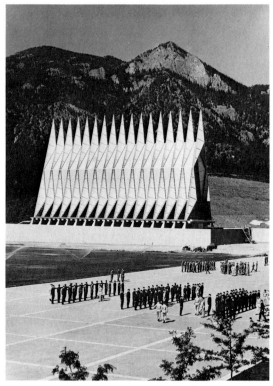

Skidmore, Owings & Merrill. U.S. Air Force Academy, Colorado Springs, Colo. 1954-58. Chapel, 1960-62

Alison and Peter Smithson; Maurice H. J. Bebb. The Economist Buildings, London, England. 1960-64. (Left: Boodles Club by J. Crunden, 1775; bay window added in 1821-24 by J.B. Papworth.)

Francis Pym. Ulster Museum Extension, Belfast, Northern Ireland. 1965-72. (Original building by James C. Wynnes, 1924.)

Gwathmey Siegel Architects. Whig Hall, Princeton University, Princeton, N.J. 1970-72. (Original building by A. Page Brown, 1893.)

tionist form seemed inadequate—indeed Mies had already proved the point with a chapel indistinguishable from his other buildings on the campus of Illinois Institute of Technology. For the Air Force the solution was a structural exercise irrationally complicated, so that a display of engineering in a pitched roof would differentiate the chapel from the other buildings and add value ("meaning") precisely because it looked—Gothic. This design aroused controversy because the "meaning" was unclear: one Congressman opposed it because he thought it looked like a wigwam.

By the end of the sixties interest in the past had been quickened by the desire to preserve nineteenth-century buildings, and has now become an economic issue as well as an aesthetic one. Even though the older buildings are not invariably distinguished, fear of what might replace them is often great enough to enlist support for their adaptation to new uses. Designing for this purpose has prompted the renewal of skills long neglected, but the uncertainty with which old buildings are remodeled is still masked by violent contrasts between the old and the new, paralleling the taste for "hybrids." Even simple and well-intentioned juxtapositions, like the Economist Buildings adjacent to the Boodles Club, betray modernism's unfamiliarity with the social graces.

We do not know what to make of the past. And even for those who balk at being deprived of memory, the act of remembering is an embarrassment that must be distanced by irony. To be taken seriously the architect must appear to be joking. The problem is to know when to laugh.

As historicizing gains momentum it strengthens the conviction that the modern movement has entered a qualitatively different phase—different from other recent manifestations that have been called "postmodern." Talbot Hamlin, writing in 1947 about "The Postmodern House," looked forward to a happier day when modernism would be over: the postmodern he anticipated was a return to the premodern. Irving Howe, writing in the sixties about American literary culture, related the postmodern to the confusions of mass society, in which the iconoclastic threat once posed by the modern is transformed into a pleasing entertainment. What is distinctively postmodern is trivialization, suggesting "the possibility that we are now living through the unsettling moral and intellectual consequences of the breakup of modernist culture, or the decline of the new."

The idea of a postmodern architecture raises the question of what is, or was, properly modern. If orthodox modernism entailed abstraction, reduction, and fidelity to structure in the service of social revolution, then its dominance as an idea ended before World War II. Defined with sufficient rigor, it is compressed to something that flashed across the horizon between the early twenties and the early thirties: 10 or 12 years and a handful of masterpieces.

Despite evidence to the contrary, most of its later style phases were not at first thought to have undermined its essential logic or its intentions, but rather to have broadened its range and its appeal. Modern architecture developed in the conviction that it had made a radical and irreparable break with the past. The accelerating emergence of historicism must now alter that view. It already has, in that the historicizing impulse naturally seeks out those phases of architectural history with which the modern senses an affinity. "History" at the moment means Neoclassicism.

Some reasons for this have been well stated by James Stirling, in his 1979 program for one of the architectural competitions conducted by the Japanese magazine *Shinkenchiku*. Stirling chose as a problem the design of a house for a famous architect — Karl Friedrich Schinkel (1781-1841). Schinkel, he explains, "was active at the time in history when austere Neoclassicism (Biedermeier) could easily have developed into modern architecture and design without a break in continuity or the intervention of the Beaux-Arts and Victorian styles. Today, as the sustaining force of the so-called abstract modern style in art, architecture, and furniture runs out of steam, we look further back than the immediate past to an architecture richer in memory and association and related to a thicker layer of history (perhaps to something similar to Soane's and Schinkel's view of Greek and Roman architecture but to Egyptian and Gothic architecture as well)."

Stirling goes on to tell the contestant that he can "assume that the competition requires a modern or Neoclassical house, or a modern Neoclassical, or classic neomodern, or any mixture of them he likes (the terms modern and Neoclassical are here used in their wider sense and are applicable to either the period of today or the period of Schinkel, or to both)."

By the time he digests the implications of this ingenious program the contestant may be ready to conclude that "modernism" was an imaginary interlude; but if it really did happen it was little more than an acute seizure of Neoclassical probity — as if architecture had been afflicted with a kind of anorexia nervosa and has just been persuaded to resume eating.

Modern architecture's affinity with Neoclassicism is real enough, but at this stage Neoclassicism, if it is not being parodied, is turned into only another mode of reductionism. What differentiates modern architecture from Neoclassicism, as from other historic styles, is its abandonment of about one-third of the resources previously available for the production of architectural form. Abstract surface and mass, and articulated structure, are retained; applied decoration, among other forms of the desirably superfluous or fictitious, is denied.

Neoclassicism retained every device: the measured deployment of all its resources enabled it to deal appropriately with every kind of situation. It could invest with dignity or liveliness even those buildings of no great intrinsic interest — low-cost housing, for example — without being obliged, as modernism has been, to distort the program by introducing gratuitous "expressive" complications or, alternatively, settling for an architecture of impoverishment. A good case can be made for Neoclassicism as a better form of modernism.

But we are not Neoclassicists, at least not yet. Modern architecture is likely to prevail because quite often it produces beautiful buildings. It is the known style, as securely entrenched as any academic mode of the nineteenth century. Abstraction still corresponds to some deeply felt need of our culture, even though it can never subdue the need for enrichment and specificity. If there is to be a major shift in sensibility it will have to overcome psychological barriers. Enrichment of form as it applies to buildings, interior decor, and furniture design need present no great problem, but typewriters, cars, and airplanes are not so tractable. Neither are those architectural situations which must accommodate technology's more intimidating artifacts. A Neoclassicical airport is imaginable, perhaps, but not without a considerable rearrangement of our prejudices.

Whatever its excesses or deficiencies, modernism has valued buildings and artifacts that are made well and do what is required of them. In that sense it has been against interpretation, preferring instead the self-evident fitness of things. As interpretation is again required, it will collide with fitness. We are still dealing with the conflict between art and technology that beset the nineteenth century, and which the modern movement expected to resolve.

Sculptural Form: Brutalism

Two architectural aesthetics vied for approval at the beginning of the sixties. One, derived from the work of Ludwig Mies van der Rohe, was concerned almost exclusively with steel and glass; it came to be widely used for high-rise buildings and other commercial work. The other derived from Le Corbusier's massively sculptural buildings in rough concrete *(béton brut)*. This post-World War II mode was often used for institutional and governmental work, perhaps because such buildings easily dominate their surround-ings. The two modes were often mixed, as they still are, and the manner of mixing them constitutes a large part of architectural history during the last 20 years. However, it is the undiluted sculptural mode that best embodies what came to be called Brutalism, notwithstanding the initial association of that term with the deliberately crude use of steel.

The buildings illustrated on pages 18 through 25 are among the most accomplished of their kind. Their aesthetic began as engineering, modified by Cubism and other modern movements in painting and sculpture. What distinguishes them from comparable

work of the twenties, besides a greater restlessness of composition, is chiefly coarse materials and finishes; the change in scale (they are often very big); and the change in purpose: they are schools, museums, theaters, shopping centers, and housing—not one is a factory, a grain silo, or a hydroelectric plant. Their architects have transformed a utilitarian aesthetic with sculptural inventions, mostly designed for aggressive effects of mass and weight.

There is a limit to the number of ways interesting sculptural events can be generated. Structure alone seldom requires bulk, but columns can be disguised or enlarged to make powerful vertical masses (1). Utility shafts are even better for this purpose, and can be topped by boxes or hoodlike projections (3). Interior stairs can make strong vertical elements, but exterior stairs, where they can be justified, are an even richer source of sculptural effects because they can introduce curves and graded shadows (3, 4, 7). If cantilevered they add a weightiness that hints of danger. Vertical and horizontal masses are often grouped side by side without seeming to touch. If they do touch they

1. Paul Rudolph. Art and Architecture Building, Yale University, New Haven, Conn. 1958-64

2. Lyons Israel Ellis Partnership. College of Engineering and Science, Polytechnic of Central London, London, England. 1963-70

3. Owen Luder. Tricorn Wholesale Market and Shopping Centre, Portsmouth, England. 1962-65

4

can be made to collide or bite pieces out of each other. Some versions of this mode owe more to Frank Lloyd Wright, de Stijl, and Constructivism than to Le Corbusier. Characteristically they have vertical and horizontal elements graded in size, thickness, color, and texture, often made to bypass each other without actually intersecting (1). This effect can make even a simple composition look quite busy. Another Wrightian variation entails the plaiting of horizontals and verticals. The horizontals dominate as cantilevered terraces with solid parapets (7, 8). These compositions tend towards lightness or calm, but this can be overcome by introducing sharp, pointed corners, inclining the parapets, and adding small but insistent detail (6).

Certain forms are thought to be inherently interesting, regardless of context. Among them is the famous "Russian Wedge," an auditorium in a wedge-shaped block (like those by Konstantin Melnikov), cantilevered in startling ways or in improbable places (2, 9). Sometimes one element, a roof for example, can be enlarged to look like a whole building, or like a wedge-shaped auditorium.

Cantilevers can make portions of a building hover in mid-air, but whole blocks can be held aloft, or made to look as if they are piled on

4, 6. Hubert Bennett; The Greater London Council. Hayward Gallery, South Bank, London, England. 1961-67

5. Patrick Hodgkinson. Brunswick Centre, Bloomsbury, London, England. 1960-72

top of each other (11). At this extreme the idea of composition itself is called into question. The parts of a building may be scattered and linked in what is meant as a dynamic, use-related conjunction, free of all prior commitments to ideas of order (12). But like aleatoric music, which in some ways it resembles, the spontaneous or random disposition of elements tends to get fixed in place—for convenience in musical performance, from necessity in architecture. The elements of what is meant to look unorganized are finally perceived as having their own order, if only because every other kind has been excluded.

7, 8. Denys Lasdun & Partners. National Theatre, South Bank, London, England. 1967-76

9. Marcel Breuer and Hamilton P. Smith. New York University Lecture Hall, University Heights Campus, New York, N.Y. 1957-61

10. Kenzo Tange. Kagawa Prefectural Gymnasium, Kagawa, Japan. 1962-64

11. Bertrand Goldberg Associates. Health Science Center, Stony Brook, N.Y. 1968-76/

12. John M. Johansen. Mummers Theater, Oklahoma City, Okla. 1966-70.

The term "megastructure" describes a gigantic building involving many different kinds of use. The type was first proposed theoretically in the eighteenth century, but for modern architecture the term is associated with one special requirement: that vertical structure alone be fixed in place, and that every other component be movable and without permanent use. Not surprisingly, the true megastructure remains a theoretical possibility only. No one needs such total flexibility; it is very expensive, and communities tend to resist building at megalomaniacal scale. Megastructure, by default, now refers either to a medium-sized building designed to look as if its components can be rearranged at will, or simply to a very large building of extended, usually linear form.

Two of the most successful built in the sixties are Paul Rudolph's Boston Government Service Center (13-15) and John Andrews's Scarborough College (16). Both are continuous linear compositions comprising at least six main units. These are differentiated from each other in response to the complex programs they serve, and some of them are further differentiated from top to bottom within themselves. At Scarborough the segments are linked by an internal street along one side, so that every part can be reached without going outdoors. The Boston Service Center was to have had an office tower as its focal point, the low line of buildings coiled around it to make a contained plaza (14). Scarborough is designed without a major vertical emphasis, but it also changes axis five times in response to its rural site. The Service Center is self-contained and, except for its tower, cannot easily be added to; the College is intended to grow by incremental additions at both ends. Rudolph's manner of introducing variety has a certain consistency throughout in the use of thin vertical piers and long horizontals, the turns or jogs being marked by curvilinear masses. Andrews marks the turns less prominently, but the segments are vertically accentuated at one end, horizontally at the other.

Both buildings skillfully demonstrate a way of coping with immense projects that, while tantalizing, is now largely rejected, in part because the giant scale that once was so exciting has come to seem overbearing and unnecessary, regardless of any practical advantages.

13-15. Paul Rudolph with Shepley, Bulfinch, Richardson & Abbott; Desmond & Lord; H. A. Dyer and Pedersen & Tilney. Boston Government Service Center, Boston, Mass. 1962-71

16. John Andrews; Page & Steele. Scarborough College, University of Toronto, Scarborough, Canada. 1963-65

16

Sculptural Form: Imagery

Twenty years ago there was growing interest in buildings that looked like some aspect of the function they served or the site they occupied. The best-known examples are Eero Saarinen's TWA Terminal and Jørn Utzon's Sydney Opera House (17, 19). To most people the Terminal looks like a bird about to take flight; the Opera House looks like billowing sails.

Both buildings were shown in a 1959 Museum of Modern Art exhibition called "Architecture and Imagery," with the observation that "to evoke such images was not necessarily the architect's intention…but the fact remains that some forms are inherently richer in overtones—are more provocative of association—than the purely geometric forms of abstract architectural composition. The images they evoke become part of a building's ultimate value whether or not the architect sought or even anticipated them."

Although Jørn Utzon was pleased to have people respond to his deliberate evocation of sails in Sydney's harbor, Eero Saarinen was reluctant to acknowledge publicly the bird-like image his building suggested, preferring to justify its shape rather by its plan and structure. Both buildings function well enough within the limits understood and accepted by the clients. But, notwithstanding their fairly explicit imagery, it is an open question as to whether enjoyment is enhanced, diminished, or left unaffected by the associations they provoke. When the image is ambiguous and probably unintended, extraneous associations may be a handicap. The larger of the two National Gymnasiums for the Olympics in Japan (18) looks like a shell when seen from the air and like a ship's prow from the ground: neither image is relevant to the site or the program. The Elephant and Rhinoceros Pavilion in London and the World of Birds building at the Bronx Zoo (20, 21) are similar in scale and texture, but not in the scale of their inhabitants. Different architects working in different cities, to accommodate different species, nevertheless shared a taste for the elephantine.

Between 1959 and 1979 speculation on imagery and its alleged importance for "meaning" has increased more than its realization in architecture. Explicit meaning derived from nonarchitectural sources seemed suspect to Saarinen because, for him as for most observers, such meaning was tied to intentions normally thought irrelevant to architecture. Not until the late sixties were buildings shaped like hats or ducks elevated to serious consideration, and for a few architects kitsch has become a quality to be sought rather than avoided. Nevertheless, it is not kitsch that generates useful overtones

17. Eero Saarinen & Associates. TWA Terminal, John F. Kennedy International Airport, New York, N.Y. 1957-62

18. Kenzo Tange. National Gymnasiums for Olympics, Tokyo, Japan. 1961-64

19. Jørn Utzon; Ove Arup & Partners; Hall, Todd & Littlemore. Sydney Opera House, Sydney, Australia. 1956-73

for architecture but rather the history of architectural styles: historicism as such now confronts this possibility more directly (see p. 155). Yet there remain differences in emotional overtones that seem inseparable from certain kinds of form.

Certain sculptural modes have been admired (or rejected) just because they are thought to be *inherently* rich, without benefit of additional, and explicit, suggestions. Thus in the thirties and forties much Scandinavian architecture, and particularly work by Alvar Aalto, combined familiar natural materials with free-flowing curves described as "organic" in acknowledgment of their compatibility with patterns of growth and human comfort. Curves were associated with "warmth." Pursued to the exclusion of everything else, such forms may become explicitly sexual and constitute a subclass of modern architecture indebted to the sculpture of Jean Arp in particular and to Surrealism in general (see p. 54).

---

20. Casson Conder & Partners. Elephant & Rhinoceros Pavilion, London Zoological Gardens, London, England. 1959-64

21. Morris Ketchum, Jr. & Associates. Lila Acheson Wallace World of Birds, Bronx Zoo, New York, N.Y. 1968-72

22. Claude Parent & Paulo Virilio. St. Bernadette of Banlay Church, Nevers, France. 1964-66

Used rather as an adjunct to rectilinearity, curved planes often enrich architectural form without necessarily becoming representational. Thus the curved corners of the Estée Lauder Laboratories (24) extend beyond the adjacent walls and then snap back into alignment: the effect makes the eye race along the wall to take the next turn; and despite its construction of modular panels, the ribbonlike wall seems to have the taut resiliency of a stretched fabric. Different kinds of movement and their concomitant associations are produced by different kinds of curves: slow and ponderous in the Rhode Island Junior College (25), rhythmically shifting and geological in the Düsseldorf playhouse (27); contemplative and sensuous in the Canadian church (26), voluptuous in the New York Synagogue (23).

23. William N. Breger. Civic Center Synagogue, New York, N.Y. 1965-67

24. Davis Brody & Associates; Richard Dattner & Associates. Estée Lauder Laboratories, Melville, N.Y. 1964-66

25. Perkins & Will; Robinson, Green & Beretta; Harkness & Geddes. Rhode Island Junior College— Knight Campus, Warwick, R. I. 1969-72

26. Douglas J. Cardinal. St. Mary's Church, Red Deer, Alberta, Canada. 1965-67

27. Bernhard M. Pfau. Düsseldorf Playhouse, Düsseldorf, Germany. 1960-69

Sculptural Form: Blank Boxes

The monumental building as a blank box used to be thought undesirable, but during the last 20 years blankness has superseded transparency in the affections of architects. Certain building types, like museums and laboratories, would seem to require few or no windows, and yet the architect can still choose to place on a building's perimeter those activities that will open it up and suggest the manner of use. (Visible escalators on the Centre Pompidou are a good example; see p. 65.) Alternatively, it may be argued that a museum *is* a kind of strongbox and should look like it, even if the look suggests that visitors may be unwelcome. The argument is not quite persuasive. It is just such public buildings that represent community effort, investment, and pride. They are not the best architectural occasions to replace welcoming speech with a blank stare.

Because surface decoration has been proscribed, unless it can be made to seem a by-product of the building process, even ornament is reduced to a matter of joints making plaids and stripes. What is left to the architect's preference is the grouping of similar boxes, or the ingenious cutting and shaping of a single box, or, finally, modifying a box so drastically as to change it to a complicated figure resembling a long-legged table, like Kisho Kurokawa's Fukuoka Bank (38); or a table with legs on top as well as below, like I. M. Pei's East Building for the National Gallery in Washington (33). Size and boldness make such buildings impressive and sometimes chillingly beautiful; always the quality of materials and craftsmanship assume great importance. Pei's East Building fascinates the eye as much by its superb masonry as by the knife-sharp corners a triangular plan imposes.

Apart from geometry there remains the structural process itself as a means of generating, or substantially influencing, the character of even a blank box. Thus the horizontal stripes on Pierluigi Spadolini's exhibition building in Florence (35) are not decoration: they are the result of building up a wall with layers of metal trays.

28. Marcel Breuer and Hamilton P. Smith. Whitney Museum of American Art, New York, N.Y. 1963-66

29. Edward Larrabee Barnes. Walker Art Center, Minneapolis, Minn. 1968-71

30. Mario J. Ciampi, Paul W. Reiter, Associate; Richard L. Jorasch, Ronald E. Wagner. University Arts Center, University of California, Berkeley, Calif. 1965-70

31. Bukichi Inoue. Ikeda Museum of 20th Century Art, Shizuoka Prefecture, Japan. 1975

32. I. M. Pei & Partners; Pederson, Hueber, Hares and Glavin. Everson Museum of Art, Syracuse, N.Y. 1962-68

33. I. M. Pei & Partners. National Gallery of Art— East Building, Washington, D.C. 1971-78

34. Marcel Breuer and Hamilton P. Smith. The Cleveland Museum of Art, Education Wing Expansion, Cleveland, Ohio. 1967-70

35. Pierluigi Spadolini. Exhibition Building, Fortezza da Basso, Florence, Italy. 1975-77

36. John Carl Warnecke & Associates. New York Telephone Company Equipment Building, New York, N.Y. 1966-72

37. Hellmuth, Obata & Kassabaum, National Air and Space Museum, Washington, D.C. 1972-76

38. Kisho Kurokawa Architect & Associates. Fukuoka Bank Headquarters Building, Fukuoka Prefecture, Japan. 1971-75

A variant on the blank-box theme is the box with a huge hole cut into it. The hole is there not so much to relieve blankness as to capitalize on effects of giant scale. The most obvious way to do this, in a building type where it is particularly effective, is to introduce two-story-high windows in a facade otherwise pierced only by monotonous windows of conventional size, as Edward Barnes did with glass-walled two-story lounge areas in his dormitories for the Rochester Institute of Technology (40). Vertical buildings with stacks of identical floors are much more difficult to vary: Arata Isozaki succeeds with his Shukosha Building because the program allowed variation in ceiling heights (41). More significant because more generally applicable is Gordon Bunshaft's astonishing tower to be built for the National Commercial Bank of Jeddah, Saudi Arabia (39). An equilateral triangle in plan, it has blank perimeter walls sheathed in travertine. Two of the three elevations are pierced by seven-story-high loggias; seven floors of glass-walled offices line their sides. The loggias shield the glass from direct sun and provide a local environment in the form of mid-air piazzas. Seen from a distance the giant openings mediate between the scale of the tower as a whole and the beehive of offices it contains, producing an image that reconciles monumentality with humane planning.

---

39. Skidmore, Owings & Merrill. National Commercial Bank (model), Jeddah, Saudi Arabia. 1977-

40. Edward Larrabee Barnes. Rochester Institute of Technology Dormitory Complex, Rochester, N.Y. 1964-67/70

41. Arata Isozaki. Shukosha Building, Fukuoka City, Japan. 1973-75

Sculptural Form: Planes and Volumes

Brutalist mass and texture, and its minimalist variants, overshadow efforts to sustain the prewar aesthetic of thin, planar surfaces screening transparent volumes. That mode of composition was once virtually synonymous with the idea of modern architecture, and yet attempts to continue it have taken on the aspect of revivalism. The buildings grouped here are by architects whose attitudes initially had this much in common: they found in French and Italian architecture prior to World War II intentions they believed still valid and still susceptible of development.

Stripped of its original "revolutionary" implications of social reorganization, this architecture depends on contrasts of planes opaque and transparent, flat and curved, and on rectilinear frameworks seemingly drawn in space, against which plastic invention can be freely deployed. In most of these buildings, and with particular refinement in Richard Meier's Saltzman and Smith houses (43, 46), internal space is both screened and revealed by the elevations. Many of these houses include rooms two or even three stories high, and the use of immense sheets of glass to make their internal relationships visible often results in dramatic extremes of scale on the elevations and excessive light within.

The style ranges from such relatively compact, simple, and prototypical buildings as Charles Gwathmey's house for his parents (45) to the extended sculpture-in-space quality of Michael Graves's Benacerraf and Snyderman houses (50, 51). The Benacerraf pavilion, added to an existing house, is also interesting for its juxtaposition of "fragments" evoking other kinds of buildings as well as Cubist painting and Constructivist sculpture.

Conspicuously different is Peter Eisenman's "House III" (48, 49). This building comprises two squares, as if one house had been rotated inside another, the walls seeming to pass through each other. The complicated and sometimes disagreeable spaces this engenders forces the occupant to "read" the structure in order to sort out the parts that belong to each square or system. The inhabi-

42. Gwathmey Siegel Architects. Tolan House, Amagansett, N.Y. 1970-71

43. Richard Meier & Associates. Saltzman House, East Hampton, N.Y. 1967-69

44. Richard Meier & Associates. Shamberg House, Chappaqua, N.Y. 1972-74

45. Gwathmey and Henderson, Architects. Gwathmey House, Amagansett, N.Y. 1965-67

46. Richard Meier & Associates. Smith House, Darien, Conn. 1965-67

47

48

49

44   Sculptural Form: Planes and Volumes

tant is required to compare bits of information meant to imply the existence of a unity that the actual field of perception contradicts, thus reversing the normal order of architectural experience. The result is something like a rigged intelligence test that the subject can only fail, even if provided with the "answers" in the form of plans, sections, isometrics, and a printed text.

Apart from such special problems, the more intricately Alexandrian such buildings become, the more they demonstrate the problematic nature of the original aesthetic, which is difficult to enrich without losing its utility and coherence.

---

47. Peter D. Eisenman. House II, Hardwick, Vt. 1968-70

48, 49. Peter D. Eisenman. House III, Lakeville, Conn. 1971-73

50. Michael Graves. Benacerraf House, Princeton, N.J. 1967-70

51. Michael Graves. Snyderman House, Fort Wayne, Ind. 1969-72

Sculptural Form: Expressionism

The angularity associated with German Expressionist art of the twenties is for many architects still an important alternative to the more static geometry of Cubism. Underlying such buildings is the intent to produce form distinguished by its dynamism rather than by its repose. Structure alone seldom justifies such forms; function, in the sense that a particular use may suggest an intensified emotional response, as in a church, may perhaps be sufficient reason. Nevertheless, even though these buildings do indeed seem charged with emotion, it is usually difficult to understand what has prompted it or how one should respond.

Hans Scharoun's Berlin Philharmonic Concert Hall is among the most successful buildings in the Expressionist genre of the last 20 years (52-54). Its auditorium and public halls are rather more persuasive than its exterior, where points, angles, and curves produce a jaunty roofline oddly unrelated to the banal windows. The combination of vertical and inclined columns in the stair hall, along with the complexity of the space itself, make it an interesting background for the movement of crowds; but a comparable deployment of space and structure in Giovanni Michelucci's Church of St. John the Baptist is difficult to relate to church ritual and seems addressed to individual anxieties rather than to the congregation (57).

This introspective quality is overcome in Portoghesi and Gigliotti's Church of the Holy Family, where a ceiling based on arcs radiating from key points in the plan clearly shapes the space in response to its significance (55). The Baroque and Hellenistic antecedents of this use of curves are more apparent in Portoghesi's Casa Baldi (56), where the advance and recession of the roofs suggests a free-hand version of the Temple of Venus at Baalbek.

Sustained restlessness is rather more difficult to achieve in large-scale public housing or multiuse buildings, but two examples from France demonstrate its feasibility. The Paris housing with its multiple cantilevers and shifting pattern of windows has the look of a twenties set for a German film—the kind of film in which the world of tomorrow is seen to be simultaneously organized, sinister, and decadent (58, 59). German cinema may also have influenced the extraordinary multipurpose building at Ville d'Ivry (60), one of two similar projects. Tiers of apartments and terraces cascading across its roof create an Expressionist village in which Dr. Caligari would have felt at home. Since this roof landscape can be seen from adjacent tall buildings, it can certainly be justified as urban entertainment, and the exterior stairs

52-54. Hans Scharoun. Philharmonic Concert Hall, Berlin, Germany. 1956-63

55. Paolo Portoghesi, Vittorio Gigliotti. Church of the Holy Family, Salerno, Italy. 1969-73

56. Paolo Portoghesi. Casa Baldi, Rome, Italy. 1959-61

57. Giovanni Michelucci. Church of St. John the Baptist, Florence, Italy. 1960-64

57

that connect many of the terraces contribute to the suggestion of an intricate casbah in which the occupants may happily lose themselves.

The Expressionist impulse is not necessarily confined to points, angles, and curves: it may also draw from Cubism. An example is Fritz Wotruba's Church of the Holy Trinity, built of massive concrete blocks piled on top of each other in what is meant to look like an almost random composition (61). In this church no single grouping of parts appears to have been repeated; but a comparable effect is achieved in the Israeli apartment house through the piling up of a few basic units, almost identical in design and placement (63); and a comparable pyramiding of forms, notched and undercut to make deep shadows, animates Walter Maria Förderer's St. Clement's Church in Switzerland (62).

In these buildings the complex forms, however pleasing they may be, are difficult to re-

58, 59. Martin S. Van Treeck. Multiuse buildings, renovation of the Ilot Riquet, Paris, France. 1972–77

60. Jean Renaudie. Jeanne-Hachette multiuse building, renovation of City Center, Ivry/Seine, France. 1969–72

50 Sculptural Form: Expressionism

late to the occasions that call them forth. A more convincing fusion of form and content occurs in Gottfried Böhm's Pilgrimage Church at Neviges, Germany (65, 67). Here the mass of the building retains its unity as a single sculpture—no doubt helped by continuing the concrete wall surfaces on to the faceted roof. The result is a brooding apparition, a ghost from the medieval past inexplicably materialized in the midst of a bourgeois townscape. And in the interior, as in many of Böhm's churches, the modulation of detail reinforces and articulates a central, overriding mood.

---

61. Fritz Wotruba. Church of the Holy Trinity, St. Georgenberg, Austria. 1965-76

62. Walter Maria Förderer. St. Clement's Catholic Church, Bettlach, Switzerland. 1963-69

63. Alfred Neumann, Zvi Hecker. Apartment building, Ramat-Gan, Israel. 1961-64

64. Walter Maria Förderer. St. Nicholas's Catholic Church, Hérémence, Switzerland. 1962-71

64

65, 67. Gottfried Böhm. Pilgrimage Church, Neviges, Germany. 1965-68

66. Gottfried Böhm. City Hall, Bensberg, Germany. 1965-67

Sculpture: Organic Form

Technology, one argument runs, should make buildings that respond to our bodies like clothing or protect them like shells. For some architects this is possible only with "irrational" curvilinear forms which avoid right angles. As interpreted by Frederick Kiesler, such forms went beyond the merely irrational to the idea of architecture as a kind of nurturing womb. He proposed houses whose interiors would have been an extension of the nervous system into a continuous warm surface. Alive with arteries for water and energy, and glowing with light from enticing tunnels and apertures, such environments anticipated the ideal of "polymorphous perversity" advocated in the early sixties by Herbert Marcuse and Norman O. Brown.

The 1960 version of Kiesler's Endless House, commissioned by The Museum of Modern Art for possible construction in its garden, used a warped concrete membrane to make "rooms," but introduced a violently textured surface (68, 69, 71). This decisive change from earlier versions moved away from the polished surfaces of technology to the gritty substance of mythological archetypes. Smoothness as an attribute of continuity still remains a theoretical possibility, as in the dreamlike vistas designed in photomontage by David Jacob (70), who worked on Eero Saarinen's TWA Terminal (17). But most design in Kiesler's organic mode follows his lead, if only because concrete sprayed on twisted metal mesh tends to be rough and to generate similar forms. Daniel Grataloup's houses in France and Switzerland are in repose, their detail small and peculiarly intimate (72-74), but Vittorio Giorgini's house in Leghorn stalks its site like a dangerous animal (76). Charles Harker's TAO Earth House looks crustacean and slightly sinister (75), not unlike Herb Greene's insectile sculpture of wood planks and shingles (77).

Interiors in this kind of building seldom equal the intense imagery of their exteriors,

68, 69, 71. Frederick Kiesler. Model for Endless House. 1960

70. David Jacob. Photomontage-model of The Continuous Room. 1960

72. Daniel Grataloup. Villa de Lyon, France. 1975–76

73, 74. Daniel Grataloup. Villa d'Anières, Geneva, Switzerland. 1970-72

74

partly because curvilinear continuity is compromised by aggressive textures, flat floors, furniture, and even the most minor use of right-angled details. Harker believes that organic sculptural form stimulates the individual's perception of wholeness, and he relates his work to Zen teachings. Günther Domenig encourages the release of creativity on the part of construction workers, who were free to modify some details of his multipurpose hall for a parochial school in Graz-Eggenberg (78). Domenig also believes that multipurpose buildings need not be "neutral" boxes: the concrete and metal mesh shell accommodates a theater, conference rooms, and dining areas in a presumably functional shape, which stands free inside a

---

75. TAO Design Group: Charles Harker, Project Architect, with Tom Lea, Evan Hintner. TAO Earth House, Austin, Tex. 1971-

76. Vittorio Giorgini: Casa Saldarini, Leghorn, Italy. 1959-60

77. Herb Greene. Architect's house, Norman, Okla. 1960-62

78. Günther Domenig; Eilfried Huth. Multipurpose hall, Graz-Eggenberg, Austria. 1973-77

courtyard. Its effect on surrounding buildings might be considered enlivening by those who do not think it disrupting. Improbable as such structures seem for anything more complicated than a house, their development would be stimulated by other technologies and, most of all, other intentions. Broader acceptance is not encouraged by anthropomorphic forms, even for private use. But characteristic alternatives now seem to derive from product design and suggest the appliance department of a discount store. Yet these designs do imply a willingness to equate "freedom" with something less idiosyncratic than self-expression.

Charles Deaton's elegant streamlined house appears poised for launching from the ridge of a Colorado mountain (79). (Its futuristic look led to its use in the film *Sleeper:* Woody Allen sought refuge here from the persecutions of tomorrow's advanced society.) Science fiction is evoked more directly by the prefabricated shell structures designed by Matti Suuronen (80, 81). "Futuro" is a 26-foot diameter spheroid made of 2-inch polyurethane foam, sandwiched between layers of fiberglass. The upper and lower hemispheres are each made in four segments, mechanically jointed and sealed, and reinforced by a steel belt. Entrance is by a retractable ladder. Three spheroids perched on a hillside suggest an invasion from outer space and could not fail to be popular with children. "Venturo" is a glass and plastic box made in increments expandable from a basic 22-foot square; its rounded corners defy structural logic but frame the views somewhat like a Chinese moon gate. U.S. manufacture of both models was discontinued in 1977 but may be resumed in 1979.

79. Charles Deaton. Architect's house, Genesee Mountain, Golden, Colo. 1963-66

80. Matti Suuronen. Casa Finlandia "Futuro," Finland. 1967-68

81. Matti Suuronen. Casa Finlandia "Venturo," Finland. 1970-71

79

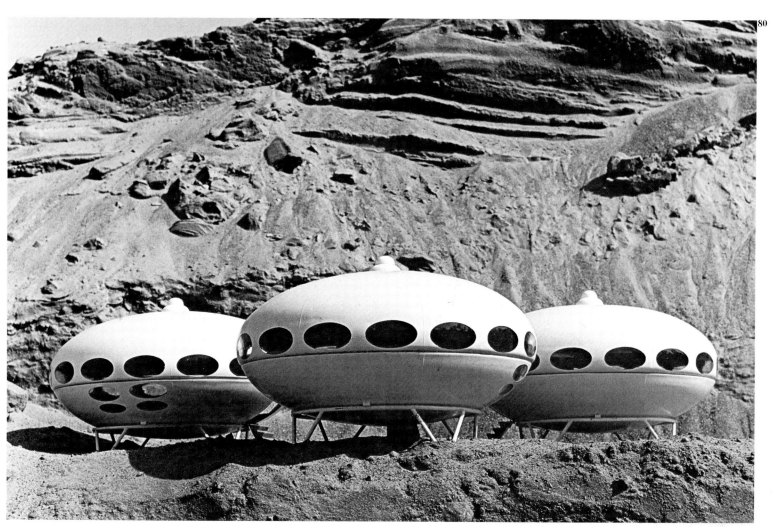

Structure: Cages

In the fifties those who believed in the objectivity of engineering thought that Mies van der Rohe's American work offered the best guide to a rational architecture. Engineering may indeed be objective and rational, but it also involves disguising aesthetic preferences to make them seem objective. What architects have in common with engineers is not simply an interest in the value of structure, but an underlying habit of thought: architecture is seen as a tangle of problems which must be sorted out, assigned priorities, and systematically solved. Once found, the solutions can be applied—or must look as if they can be applied—everywhere. More valuable than the result is systematic application itself.

The paradigmatic problem of architecture as pure structure is simply a flat roof at giant span; and the definitive solution is Mies's Berlin Museum, with its 214-foot-square roof of steel coffers carried by two columns on each elevation (82). In manipulating this theme the roof slab can be raised or lowered on prominent or inconspicuous columns; cantilevered or supported at its perimeter; thickened for structural or mechanical reasons; or even used as an attic. (Variations prompted by "meaning" are discussed on p. 118.) Divorced from other design entanglements, its extreme development is the deep space-frame spanning immense distances; at Simon Fraser University the space-frame has a transparent covering and shelters an open-air campus center (86).

Some multistory buildings are simply stacks of flat roofs, horizontality being emphasized by columns kept well behind the perimeter. At the Weyerhaeuser office building, although it is difficult to tell from the photograph, each floor slab is set back from the one below (87). Because the columns are placed on a grid diagonal to the building's perimeter, each setback exposes another range of columns out of alignment with those in front. The structure has the abstract purity of a diagram but yields an unexpectedly animated effect.

Abstraction is reinforced by eliminating metal frames around the glass, as in the IBM World Trade Headquarters and the Design Research Showroom (88, 89). Much of the effect depends on maintaining transparent corners; the Design Research building introduces some extra ones. Both versions also depend on broad, unbroken fascias, but the fascia may be used for decorative purposes. At the Out-Patient Clinics in San Francisco thin slabs extend beyond the glass and are enlivened, on two elevations, by the exposed ends of concrete joists (90): the dotted line

they make recalls comparable details in timber architecture.

The horizontality of these multistory buildings continues ideas developed in the twenties, or earlier, when horizontality was valued because it expressed the strength of new materials. Better still, it had no classical precedent. Today it recalls the precedent of the twenties because the debate as to whether a skyscraper should stress verticality or horizontality (or both, on different sides of the same building) was temporarily settled in favor of horizontality.

The natural resolution is a structural cage in which horizontal and vertical elements are equally apparent, but with horizontals dominating simply as a result of making the true proportions of the cage visible. The BMA Tower is an unusually abstract and probably definitive version (91). Its cage stands free of the walls; distinctions between columns and

82. Ludwig Mies van der Rohe. New National Gallery, Berlin, Germany, 1962-68

83. I. M. Pei & Partners. National Airlines Terminal, John F. Kennedy International Airport, New York, N.Y. 1960-70

84. Skidmore, Owings & Merrill. Noxell Corporation Headquarters, Cockeysville, Md. 1966-67

85. Arne Jacobsen. Landskrona Sports Hall, Landskrona, Sweden. 1961-64

86. Erickson-Massey. Simon Fraser University, Burnaby, British Columbia, Canada. 1963-65

87. Skidmore, Owings & Merrill. Weyerhaeuser Headquarters, Tacoma, Wash. 1967-71

88. Edward Larrabee Barnes. IBM World Trade/Americas Far East Corporation Headquarters, Mt. Pleasant, N.Y. 1971-75

89. Benjamin Thompson & Associates, Inc. Design Research Showroom, Cambridge, Mass. 1968-69

90. Reid & Tarics Associates. Out-Patient Clinics Building and Parking Structure, University of California Medical Center, San Francisco, Calif. 1969-72

beams are minimized, and both are sheathed in white marble. The proportions make just those horizontal slots Mies disliked, but which he overcame by introducing a secondary structure of vertical mullions, ostensibly to hold the glass but in reality to assert the preeminence of verticality.

Chicago's Civic Center continues Mies's concern with structural articulation but accepts an even greater exaggeration of the horizontal dimension brought about by new high-strength steel alloys, which here increased the span between columns to 87 feet (92). Other ways of changing scale are seen in the University of Illinois Administration Building, where perimeter columns vary in size and number as the building rises (93), and in Pittsburgh's U.S. Steel building, which consists of a steel cage in three-story increments with a second set of lighter steel frames inside each section (96). A development of some importance to the economic use of steel is the diagonal bracing seen on Chicago's John Hancock building, which is more happily distinguished by its taper (94). The scale of the diagonals converts the building into an artifact of civil engineering, like a bridge, and produces unfortunate effects on interior space. More interesting is the cluster of nine towers for the Sears building, at 110

91. Skidmore, Owings & Merrill. BMA Tower, Kansas City, Mo. 1961-64

92. C. F. Murphy Associates; Skidmore, Owings & Merrill; Loebl, Schlossman, Bennett & Dart. Chicago Civic Center, Chicago, Ill. 1960-66

93. Skidmore, Owings & Merrill. Administration Building, University of Illinois, Circle Campus, Chicago, Ill. 1962-65

94. Skidmore, Owings & Merrill. John Hancock Center, Chicago, Ill. 1965-70

95. Skidmore, Owings & Merrill. Sears Tower, Chicago, Ill. 1972-74

96. Harrison and Abramovitz and Abbe. U.S. Steel Corporation Headquarters, Pittsburgh, Pa. 1968-71

97. Skidmore, Owings & Merrill. Marine Midland Building, New York, N.Y. 1965-68

98. Muchow Associates. Park Central Building, Denver, Colo. 1970-73

98

stories currently the world's tallest (95). Each tower is a tube 70 feet square, with closely spaced perimeter columns. Rising to different heights, the tubes make an asymmetrical composition of great interest, but of course the same massing can be achieved by more conventional engineering.

In the sixties attention gradually returned to the design of the skin concurrent with the design of structure. Economy prompted simplification, and one of the most important solutions was found in 140 Broadway in New York (97). This building looks like a package printed with two different kinds of black ink —shiny and matte. Its flat surface has often been repeated, with minor variations, and in most of them the cage is a kind of ghost image on a dark surface. Surprisingly, there have been few attempts to vary the profile and massing of the package itself, as is done in the Denver office building (98).

At another level of structural design, the cage is subjected to substantial dislocations. When enthusiasm for structure is no longer satisfied with abstraction and reduction, attention shifts to details of joinery and the multiplication of parts. Thus the bones of structure may assume dinosaur proportions, or joints may swell like arthritic knuckles. The opposite impulse toward structural elaboration replaces mass with line, introducing cables, pipes, and ducts. Probably the most engaging example of this overscaled hardware is the Centre National d'Art et de Culture Georges Pompidou, popularly known as the Beaubourg (101–03). This building accommodates museum, library, restaurant, and performance facilities. Its structure combines cast-steel tubes and joints with tension cables, leaving the interiors free of columns. Corridors and escalators in plastic tubes are suspended along the main elevation; the rear elevation offers a display of ducts painted in primary colors, suggesting a stylish petroleum refinery. Unfortunately the tension members contribute to low-level vibration, and exposed ducts make the interiors difficult to use as art galleries; but the structure does achieve ingenious "problem-solving" complications that would be lacking in a conventional steel or concrete cage.

99. Samuel Glaser Associates; Kallmann & McKinnell. Government Center Garage, Boston, Mass. 1966-70

100. William Kessler & Associates Inc. Center for Creative Studies, College of Art and Design, Detroit, Mich. 1971-75

101-03. Piano & Rogers; Ove Arup & Partners. Centre National d'Art et de Culture Georges Pompidou, Paris, France. 1971-77

101

102

103

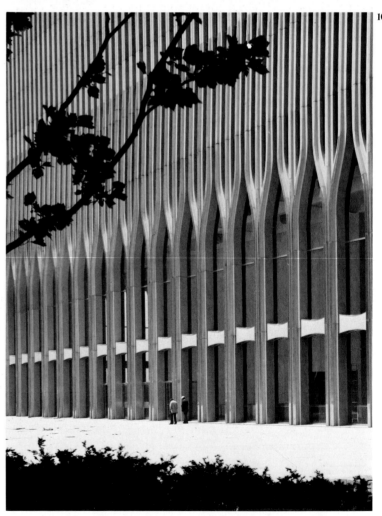

The pure cage may be the clearest and most logical of structures, but it is not necessarily the most efficient and certainly it is no longer the most interesting for architects to design. Some of the alternatives can be divided into three groups. In the first, numerous perimeter columns are closely spaced to make what might almost be a load-bearing wall, as in One Shell Plaza and the World Trade Center (106, 107). In the former the concrete piers are thick and thin, expanded and contracted in response to structural stresses. Another variation, even more fine-grained and evenly textured, is the wall designed as a flat truss for the Pittsburgh IBM Building (108).

A second theme involves the clustering of vertical shafts, sometimes for support and sometimes for surface effect. On the Marina City apartment houses they are a graceful surface modulation achieved by the repetition of curved balconies (109).

A third motif deals with corners: four cylinders with floors suspended between them for the Knights of Columbus building (105); or the ends of a rectangular building treated as pylons, with the floors stretching between them, as in the Federal Reserve Bank of Boston (104). Both versions dramatically alter the petty scale and monotony of conventional high-rise elevations, yet just this improvement has been criticized for introducing an element of "gargantuan" scale. Undoubtedly the use of this motif in the urban context is disruptive, though perhaps to greater advantage than the pseudo-megastructure from which it derives. At the same time what might be its greatest advantage on a city street—its usefulness in turning corners—remains relatively unexplored.

---

104. Hugh Stubbins and Associates. Federal Reserve Bank of Boston, Boston, Mass. 1972-78

105. Kevin Roche John Dinkeloo & Associates. Knights of Columbus Headquarters Building, New Haven, Conn. 1965-70

106. Skidmore, Owings & Merrill. One Shell Plaza, Houston, Tex. 1969-71

107. Minoru Yamasaki and Associates; Emery Roth & Sons. The World Trade Center, New York, N.Y. 1962-75

108. Curtis & Davis. IBM Building, Pittsburgh, Pa. 1962-64

109. Bertrand Goldberg Associates. Marina City, Chicago, Ill. 1960-64

Structure: Cantilevers

Buildings can be made to hover in mid-air, span voids like bridges, or leap out of themselves into space. The effects are sculptural; the means are structural. The cantilever is the essential technique for all manner of structural excess.

Skyscrapers are the least likely beneficiaries of this kind of design, because cantilevering requires massive core supports and tends to reduce the amount of usable floor space. An extreme development is the Shizuoka Shinbun branch office (115), which occupies a minute site at the intersection of an elevated expressway and several busy thoroughfares in Tokyo. Small units containing offices are projected from a cylinder (which contains utilities and an elevator), and it is clear that the desire to cantilever takes precedence over practical considerations. The building for the University of Paris (116), on the other hand, engages a similar theme but is obliged to accommodate larger areas of usable space. The compromise is effected by a combination of concrete shafts from which the floors are cantilevered, but which remain largely concealed from view, with adjacent concrete shafts providing supplementary support and creating the illusion that the glazed volumes are hung from them.

Constructivist projects of the twenties are recalled by two art museums and an administration building (112–14). The latter uses towers, approximately square in plan, bridged at different levels and in different directions by two-story-high square tubes. These horizontal elements appear to be cantilevered beyond the towers, but are actually suspended by rigid tension members. The American art museum is less dramatic for the technical aspects of its structure than for its elevated plaza framed by the building itself. This composition is meant to terminate a vista, but its scale—as with most such exercises—overwhelms everything around it.

The University of California Library (111) employs cantilevered concrete bents like those used for stadiums. The Spanish tower (110) conceals its structure, rotating alternate floors to make projecting corners. Between the bands of windows the space is filled by warped surfaces that look as if they had stretched like rubber as the floors were turned.

---

110. Miguel Fisac. Jorba Laboratories, Madrid, Spain. 1965-67

111. William L. Pereira Associates. Central University Library, University of California, San Diego, Calif. 1966-70

112. I. M. Pei & Partners. Herbert F. Johnson Museum of Art, Cornell University, Ithaca, N.Y. 1968-73

113. State Roads Offices for Engineering and Administration, Tbilisi, Georgia, U.S.S.R. 1977

114. Arata Isozaki. Kitakyushu City Museum of Art, Kitakyushu City, Japan. 1971-74

115. Kenzo Tange & Urtec Team. Shizuoka Shinbun Branch Office, Tokyo, Japan. 1966-67

116. Andrault & Parat. University of Paris, Faculté de Tolbiac, Paris, France. 1971-73

117

118

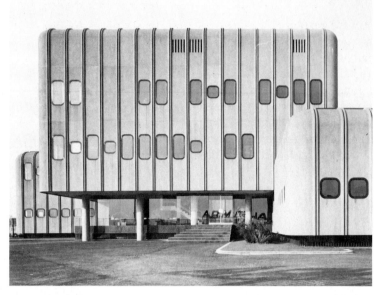

119

120

121

122

Structure: Design by System

Architecture conceived as the design of structural details tends to follow a specific pattern of development. Whether the structure being designed is the system of primary supports or the lightweight cladding, it is developed from a single component. Once the component is designed, the entire building is designed—the component need only be multiplied ad infinitum. Architecture then becomes little more than the replication of a detail.

Sometimes such components embrace more than a single element, as is the case with the window-walls of the Philadelphia Police Headquarters (117). Here each stack of three windows is a single precast concrete frame, like a ladder or a perforated pier, carrying the floor slabs. Walls on the Arm Italia industrial buildings (118) are built of comparable vertical elements, but here the window pattern is varied to great advantage.

The Banque Lambert building in Brussels (119) treats columns as sharp spikes or prongs, extended below and above the floor slabs. The BMW Garage (120) is based on essentially the same idea, but here the fascia of each slab is enlarged to make a massive parapet, while the "columns" projecting above and below are reduced to stumps.

The preceding examples are instances of rational problem-solving arbitrarily inflected toward sculptural qualities, which may or may not be at variance with structural logic. The intention has been to make structure in some way "expressive"—but not necessarily of a structural fact. Another response within the parameters of problem-solving treats the skin of a building like a precisely machined industrial artifact, and goes to some trouble to emphasize the resemblance.

Thus the metal panels of the Kiln Farm building (121) look like the stamped sides of oil cans, or like panels on the tractor parked in front of it. Individual segments are punched out to make windows whose rounded corners are an essential part of the pattern; round-cornered windows in the Bronx medical facility (122) recall windows on buses and trains, but remain architectural. In the IBM building in Hamburg (123) rounded corners are used to blunt the contours of a volume, rather than to generate an overall pattern, and suggest such large-scale artifacts as automobiles and airplanes. Here the whole is more than the sum of its parts, problem-solving having been used to make a preconceived shape.

117. Geddes, Brecher, Qualls, and Cunningham. Police Headquarters Building, Philadelphia, Pa. 1959-62

118. Angelo Mangiarotti. Arm Italia Factory, Cinisello Balsamo, Italy. 1970-72

119. Skidmore, Owings & Merrill. Banque Lambert, Brussels, Belgium. 1957-65

120. Karl Schwanzer. BMW Motor Co. Employee Parking Garage, Munich, Germany. 1968-70

121. Derek Walker with Industry Group at Milton Keynes Development Corp. System Building for Industry (at Kiln Farm), Milton Keynes, England. 1971-72

122. Richard Meier & Associates. Bronx Developmental Center, New York, N.Y. 1970-76

123. Dissing & Weitling. IBM Branch Office and Data Processing Center, Hamburg, Germany. 1973-77

125

126

Structure: Glass Skins

The mystical properties of light and transparency, according to German enthusiasts at the beginning of this century, would lead to a glass architecture of literally redemptive powers. More prosaically, Mies van der Rohe noted (in connection with his 1922 study for a glass skyscraper) that the significant thing about glass was the play of reflections, not shadows, and so the curved walls shown in his model (127) are meant to reflect each other rather than respond to some functional requirement of the plan. The plan itself showed no columns, the structure being of no great concern to Mies at that time. But in subsequent work it was the skeletal structure he focused on, finally excluding almost everything else, and it was transparency, not reflections, that helped to emphasize the regular disposition of the structural cage. In this context reflections have no advantage, and Mies's most persuasive buildings are not his skyscrapers, with their dark glass backed by dark curtains or blinds, but those one-room structures whose clear glass maintains total transparency.

It has taken almost 50 years for architecture to return to Mies's earlier notions of the primacy of surface, and this time the object is to conceal rather than reveal. Tinted glass has been widely used since the fifties to reduce glare and heat load. Mirror glass for buildings was first developed for the Bell Telephone Laboratories Research Center (124), at the prompting of Eero Saarinen and his associates Kevin Roche and John Dinkeloo. Glass can be tinted *and* mirrored, and both kinds are now often combined, but it is the technique of mirroring that has brought to the glass facade a degree of abstraction that is without precedent.

When glass was first used to make the entire surface of a building—not just its windows—it was held in place by highly visi-

ble metal armatures. More recently, however, the desire to maintain perfect continuity of surface has led to the refinement of the joints, which now are made as flush with the surface as possible and often with flexible synthetics rather than metal frames. Sheets of glass can also be fastened to each other by metal clasps (125).

Glass technology, and the skill with which it is used, varies from one country to another, but nowhere is it more sophisticated than in England—perhaps after all elegance comes more readily to the English temperament than Brutalism. An example is the Century House building (126), a facade between other buildings on a city street. Its assembly system, called Astrowall, is a commercial product which leaves little initiative to the architect. At Century House the glass divisions include a visible black gasket and, down the center of each square, a nearly invisible hairline where the glass has been butted and sealed with a translucent joint.

Glass cladding systems have accelerated the mass production of buildings whose design is largely determined not only by the manufacturers of glass and its assembly systems, but also by developers and financial institutions. An architect is scarcely required. For the cheaper sort of building he is expected to provide a decent entrance and to see to it that the internal distribution of services does not interfere with maximum rentable space.

The package quality of such buildings, and the speed with which they can be designed and built, is in some respects the fulfillment of what was thought desirable in the twenties. It was then supposed that technology, if properly mastered, could produce an architecture so pervasive that it would become an industrial vernacular. In those terms, excellent work could be guaranteed simply by following established procedures, while refinements of design could be left to a few specialists. In practice it is often just those buildings that add nothing to the production

124. Eero Saarinen & Associates. Bell Telephone Laboratories, Research Center, Holmdel, N.J. 1957-62

125. Smith, Hinchman & Grylls Associates Inc. Architects' office building, Detroit, Mich. 1971-72

126. Raymond J. Cecil. Century House office building, London, England. 1973-75

127. Ludwig Mies van der Rohe. Model, Glass Skyscraper Project. 1922

128. Hellmuth, Obata & Kassabaum. The Equitable Building, St. Louis, Mo. 1969-71

129. Erickson-Massey. Canadian Government Pavilion, Expo '70, Osaka, Japan. 1967-69

130. Leonard S. Parker. Gelco Corporation International Headquarters, Eden Prairie, Minn. 1974-75

process, and therefore look least designed, that are the most convincing (128).

What is surprising is that glass itself, a material inseparable from modern architecture, should be so retarded in comparison with other materials and technologies. Glass block, for example, although popular in the thirties and forties, was abandoned by architects because few companies were willing to solve its many technical problems. Except for minor variations, the same block designs first developed 30 or more years ago are still the only ones available, and architects today sometimes use them to evoke a thirties aura. Experimentation now takes place largely in countries with more flexible production systems.

The Japanese university building (132) uses preassembled steel frames with small, amber-colored glass blocks whose circular centers recall the blocks manufactured in France during the twenties and used by Pierre Chareau and Le Corbusier. In Buenos Aires several bank buildings and their interiors (133, 134, inside front cover) are remarkable for their use of brilliant color: blue for the Urquiza branch, amber yellow for the decorative walls of the Condor branch, and a glowing red-orange for the interior of the Headquarters. This latter is a faceted glass shell built inside an existing structure. Floors, ceilings, and walls are all made of glass blocks in steel frames, some of them removable for access to concealed lighting. An alternative to glass block was used in the Hall of Science built for the 1964 New York World's Fair (131). Here a continuous undulating wall is made of a concrete grid filled with irregular chunks of colored glass.

131. Harrison and Abramovitz. Museum of Science and Technology, New York World's Fair, 1964, New York, N.Y. 1963-64

132. Fumihiko Maki. School of Art and Physical Education, Tsukuba University, Tsukuba Newtown, Japan. 1973-74

133. Manteola, Petchersky, Sanchez-Gomez, Santos, Solsona, Viñoly. Condor Branch, Bank of the City of Buenos Aires, Argentina. 1971

134. Manteola, Petchersky, Sanchez-Gomez, Santos, Solsona, Viñoly. Villa Urquiza Branch, Bank of the City of Buenos Aires, Argentina. 1969

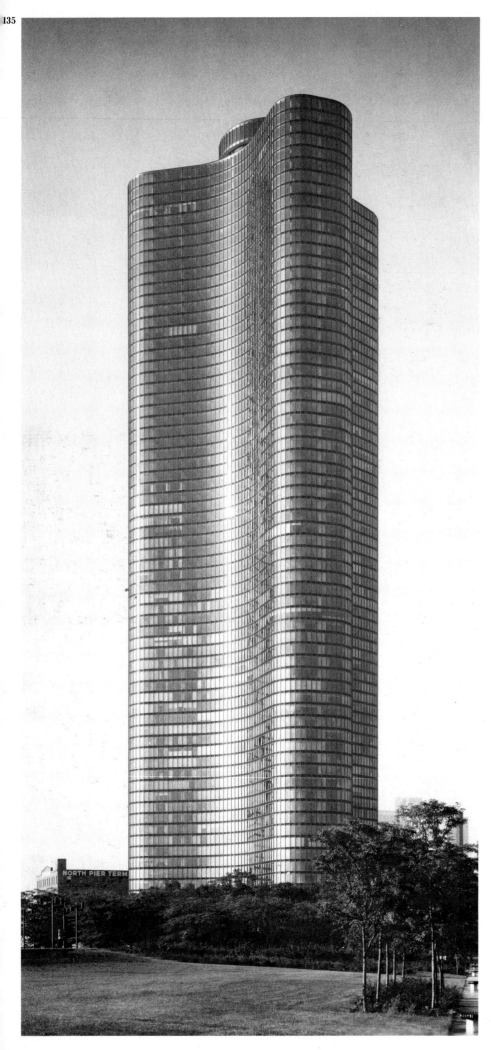

135. Schipporeit-Heinrich. Lake Point Tower apartment house, Chicago, Ill. 1964-68

136. José Antonio Coderch y de Sentmenat. Office buildings, Barcelona, Spain. 1965-72

137. Harrison and Abramovitz. Phoenix Mutual Life Insurance Building, Hartford, Conn. 1960-64

138. William L. Pereira Associates. Great Western Savings Center, Beverly Hills, Calif. 1969-73

139. Arthur Erickson/Mathers & Haldenby. New Massey Hall (model), Toronto, Canada. 1977-

The Willis Faber & Dumas office building is the most sophisticated exercise in glass technology yet seen (although it may soon be rivaled by the flexible glass roof of Massey Hall, 139). In many ways it is the belated realization of ideas first put forward by Mies, most obviously in its curved wall like a palisade following the contours of the site. Apart from that configuration, however, it achieves effects of scalelessness Mies renounced.

The wall is divided into facets, each facet comprising six panels of glass. These are bolted to each other with metal patches at the corners. Each ribbon of six panels is suspended from the roof by means of a single bolt and a metal clamp to spread the weight. The joints are closed with a translucent, flexible silicone sealant. Lateral stiffening is provided by glass fins suspended from the ceilings in flexible mounts. A damaged panel of glass can be (and has been) unbolted and easily replaced without affecting the adjacent panels.

Other refinements of this building are a roof covered with grass and a toplighted central circulation area equipped with escalators, which, like other mechanical installations scattered throughout the building, rejoice in exhibiting their working parts.

The purity of the glass wall system is an extreme development of Mies's "less is more" philosophy. But once away from the glass, that attitude is superseded by a kind of *laissez-faire*, whereby separate systems—for sound control, circulation, mechanical services, lighting—are allowed highly visible presences but are seldom allowed to touch. It is this additive character that makes the building a three-dimensional catalog of ingenious solutions to problems of which, otherwise, one might not have been aware. Problem-solving replaces "expression."

140–44. Foster Associates. Offices for Willis Faber & Dumas Ltd., Ipswich, England. 1970–75

145

146

147

Before the advent of tinted glass the alternation of solid spandrel and transparent window made surface continuity difficult to achieve. Dark glass increases reflectivity and thus improves surface continuity; but mirror glass achieves near-perfect continuity because it eliminates any disruption from within the building—at least until the lights go on at night.

The aesthetic motive is the decisive one, but the energy crisis has added economic incentives favoring mirrored glass skins. Such facades make no distinction between window openings and the much larger areas of solid wall that are often concealed behind the reflecting glass. From within, the glass is transparent, but the observer outside cannot tell which panels of mirror are in fact real windows. Consequently windows may be reduced in size, which reduces heating and cooling costs, and may be placed without regard for external appearance. The more

145. Cesar Pelli, Partner-in-Charge of Design; Gruen Associates. Pacific Design Center, West Hollywood, Calif. 1971-76

146. 3D/International. Century Center Office Building, San Antonio, Tex. 1971-72

147. Odell Associates Inc. North Carolina Blue Cross and Blue Shield Headquarters, Chapel Hill, N.C. 1968-73

148. 3D/International. Century Center Office Building #5, Atlanta, Ga. 1973-74

149. Shoei Yoh. Ingot Coffee Shop, Kitakyushu-shi, Japan. 1977

regular the grid, the more abstract the elevations. Perfect regularity results in perfect meaninglessness, except that the whole conveys an indifference to human presence most people interpret as hostile. Moreover, imperfections in the glass, and alignments that can never be truly accurate, sometimes fragment the reflected image. The result is an irritating display of failed perfection.

What makes mirror buildings so fascinating is their combination of calculated technique with accidents of light. Given the right moment, they are even more photogenic than other kinds of modern architecture. The right moment usually occurs before or after a rainstorm—or at dawn or twilight. High noon on a cloudless day may be only blinding, or dull gray: stormy weather is best, and mirror buildings are perhaps most rewarding in the open countryside. In town they usually damage what they most depend upon: the environment they reflect. And in town they can be as unsociable as a conversation with someone wearing mirrored sunglasses: when the other person's eyes are not visible one feels at a disadvantage.

Although glass technology may develop further—to explore color, texture, and translucency as well as reflections—at its present stage architects have preferred to concentrate on a building's shape. Clover leaves (135, 136), lozenges and ovoids (137, 138), parallelograms, pyramids, cylinders, and cubes proliferate and are all for the most

150, 152. Kevin Roche John Dinkeloo & Associates. College Life Insurance Company of America Headquarters, Indianapolis, Ind. 1967-71

151, 153. Johnson/Burgee; S. I. Morris Associates. Pennzoil Place, Houston, Tex. 1970-76

154. Peterson and Brickbauer Inc.; Brown, Guenther, Battaglia, Galuin. Blue Cross Blue Shield of Maryland Inc., Towson, Md. 1970-72

152

153

154

part equally arbitrary. But is there something wrong with being arbitrary? Or is it only that extreme precision—objectivity in its technological dress—implies a loftier purpose than the making of curious shapes?

The three modified pyramids for a life insurance company (150, 152) are perhaps a symbolically appropriate environment in which to anticipate death: enjoying them, however, depends in large part on the way they change relationship as one moves around them, an effect even more intensely developed by the twin office buildings of Pennzoil Place (151). These are works whose shapes do not depend on glass. In many cases glassiness is made even more startling because the shapes derive from masonry architecture. Thus the Fort Worth National Bank (158), with its chamfered corners and its sloping base, and the clustered towers of the Bonaventure Hotel in Los Angeles (166) recall the fortified castles Louis Kahn retrieved for his masonry buildings (and for a glass building as well, in at least one project). Recall is also involved in the Hyatt Regency Hotel (163, 164) in Dearborn, Michigan, a building whose stepped rear facade in a "dynamic" thirties manner is more interesting than its monumentally bland entrance— and which anticipated the still more elaborately busy massing of the Hyatt Regency Hotel in Dallas (165 and inside front cover).

Even when these forms do not remind us of ancient history, they cannot escape the history of modern architecture. But long low buildings of dark or mirrored glass, unlike skyscrapers, are less evocative of a historic type from which they deviate. The Pacific Design Center suggests to most people an extrusion that could well have been even longer, but the effectiveness of its length depends on simultaneously seeing the varied profile of its end elevation (145). The Century Center Office Building is rather like a carton with one flap lifted (146). Actually this inclined wall conceals a four-story-high space serving as lobby and corridor, overlooked by the offices. Again, it is the end elevation that makes the building intelligible. These configurations suggest that a building of reflective glass can be made more interesting when it is feasible to treat one elevation as if it were a cross-section, disclosing something of its internal organization.

---

155. I. M. Pei & Partners, Henry N. Cobb, Design Partner. John Hancock Tower, Boston, Mass. 1967-76

156. Johnson/Burgee; Edward F. Baker Associates, Inc. I.D.S. Center, Minneapolis, Minn. 1968-73

157. Skidmore, Owings & Merrill. Equibank Building, Pittsburgh, Pa. 1973-76

158. John Portman & Associates. Fort Worth National Bank, Fort Worth, Tex. 1969-74

159. Kevin Roche John Dinkeloo & Associates. United Nations Plaza Hotel and Office Building, New York, N.Y. 1969-75

160. K. R. Cooper. Offices for Ontario Hydro, Toronto, Canada. 1972-76

161. John Brunton & Partners. Europa House office building, Hull, England. 1973-75

162. Curtis L. Beattie, Designer/Project Architect with Chester L. Lindsey Architects. Fourth & Vine Office Building, Seattle, Wash. 1973-75

163, 164. The Luckman Partnership. Hyatt Regency Hotel, Dearborn, Mich. 1972-76

165. Welton Becket Associates. Hyatt Regency Hotel and Reunion Tower, Dallas, Tex. 1973-78

166. John Portman & Associates. Los Angeles Bonaventure Hotel, Los Angeles, Calif. 1970-76

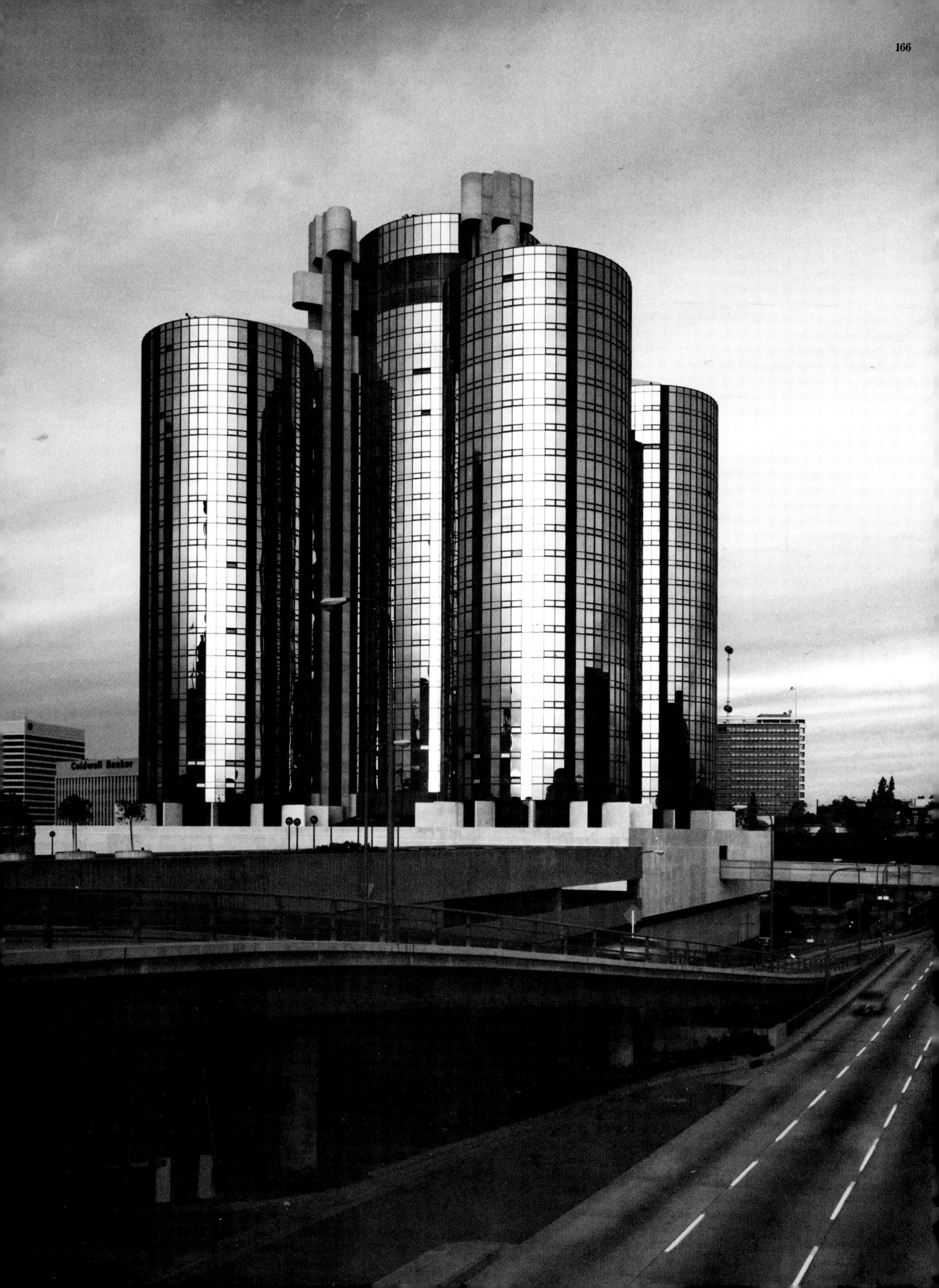
Coldwell Banker

Greenhouses and Other Public Spaces

The building with a glass roof as well as glass walls may be the type toward which modern architecture aspires, but few architects have had the opportunity to build it. When it does get built it seems to require so much metal structure that it looks like a steel cage rather than a glass volume. This quality has been deliberately emphasized in the Niagara Falls Winter Garden (167, 168), where several levels of structural articulation are combined; it is minimized, or at least regularized, by the continuous space frame used for the Garden Grove Community Church (170), now in construction.

Greenhouse buildings can yield vast, light-filled interiors in fulfillment of a nineteenth-century dream. No Crystal Palace could equal the fantasy of Buckminster Fuller's dome at Montreal's Expo 67, or of Japan's Summerland recreation center (174), or for that matter the more subtly internalized world of the Deere & Company annex (172), an office building whose lush gardens and intricate vistas make it seem like a private community.

Competing with the public space as a light-filled garden—on the model first developed for the Ford Foundation (175, 176)—is an image related to the disquieting moods of Expressionism, science fiction, and the abiding Piranesian delight in places that look, and may in fact be, slightly dangerous. But no one visiting any of the astonishing hotels designed by John Portman is in danger, unless he misses his footing while staring upward at the dizzying display of balconies, elevators, bridges, canopies, sculptures, and, in the Renaissance Center Plaza Hotel (182), trees in tubs cantilevered from columns.

These hotel lobbies unexpectedly reintroduced significant interior space as a commercially viable entity—indeed their very extravagance has ensured their commercial success. No museum or concert hall rivals their lavish architectural incident. They now constitute tourist attractions in their host cities and are among the few buildings of the last two decades that can claim to have a genuine popular following. Portman has made it clear that in certain circumstances too much is barely enough; the most dramatic of his hotel interiors are counterparts of Charles Garnier's Paris Opera, and enjoy a comparable success.

167, 168. Cesar Pelli, Partner-in-Charge of Design; Gruen Associates. Rainbow Center Mall and Winter Garden, Niagara Falls, N.Y. 1976-78

169. Ole Meyer. Bella Center, trade mart & exhibition building, Copenhagen, Denmark. 1973-75

170. Johnson/Burgee. Garden Grove Community Church (model), Garden Grove, Calif. 1977-

Elements of Portman's rhetorical style can be found in other kinds of commercial and governmental structures. The Buenos Aires Bank of London and South America makes do with what must be one of Argentina's most imposing stairs (180); the simple forms of the open-walled but transparent-roofed court in Mexico City's Government Building are monumental, but ceremoniously calm (181).

These are exceptional spaces, and to some extent all such giant public spaces are exceptional; yet one type may well become ubiqui-

---

171. Kevin Roche John Dinkeloo & Associates. Irwin Union Bank & Trust Company, Columbus, Ind. 1966–72

172. Kevin Roche John Dinkeloo & Associates. Deere & Company, West Office Building, Moline, Ill. 1975–78

173. Takenaka Komuten Co. Ltd. Design Dept.; Takao Kohira. Nagashima Tropical Garden, Mie Prefecture, Japan. 1967–68

174. Ishimoto Architectural & Engineering Firm, Inc.: Kinji Fukuda, Project Architect, Minoru Murakami, Architect. Summerland recreation center, near Tokyo, Japan. 1966–67

tous and certainly has influenced other kinds of buildings. The shopping center with its glass-roofed street, like the greenhouse, elaborates a nineteenth-century ideal. It is in this extended rather than compacted kind of space that modern architecture promptly encounters its characteristic difficulty: the invention of incident and the sequential ordering of space when the program will not afford, and the architect will not allow, any fictive devices. We must then accept infinite extension, relieved only by hanging plants and ornaments (184), or we may be satisfied with ducts and plumbing brought out of retirement to festoon the walls (183, 189).

175, 176. Kevin Roche John Dinkeloo & Associates. The Ford Foundation Headquarters Building, New York, N.Y. 1963-67

177. Johnson/Burgee; Edward F. Baker Associates, Inc. I.D.S. Center, Minneapolis, Minn. 1968-73

178. John Portman & Associates. Hyatt Regency Hotel, Atlanta, Ga. 1963-67

179. John Portman & Associates. Hyatt Regency Hotel, San Francisco, Calif. 1968-73

180. Estudio Sanchez Elia — Peralta Ramos, Bank of London & South America, Buenos Aires, Argentina. 1961-66

181. Teodoro González de León; Abraham Zabludovsky; Jaime Ortiz Monasterio; Luis Antonio Zapiain. Government Building, Cuauhtemoc District, Mexico City, Mexico. 1972-74

182. John Portman & Associates. Renaissance Center, Detroit, Mich. 1971-77

189

183. Bregman & Hamann; Zeidler Partnership. Toronto Eaton Centre, Toronto, Canada. 1973-77

184. Hellmuth, Obata & Kassabaum. The Galleria shopping center, Houston, Tex. 1967-69

185. John Carl Warnecke & Associates; Peterson, Clark & Associates. Hennepin County Government Center, Minneapolis, Minn. 1968-76

186. Sachio Otani. Kawaracho high-rise apartment house, Kawasaki, Japan. 1970-74

187. I. M. Pei & Partners. National Gallery of Art — East Building, Washington, D.C. 1971-78

188. Cossutta & Associates. Crédit Lyonnais Tower, offices and Hotel Frantel, Lyons, France. 1972-74

189. Schoeler Heaton Harvor Menendez. Charlebois High School, Ottawa, Canada. 1971-72

Hybrids

Different architectural effects are normally pursued separately, one at a time. When they cross over and modify each other we expect some effort toward unification. What is surprising is to see unrelated modes handled separately in one and the same building.

Among the most interesting work of the sixties is a multiuse building in Rome that juxtaposes commercial space in a glass-walled box with a topping of Constructivist concrete beams and parapets for private apartments (192). The contrast between top and bottom is made even more emphatic by their different alignments in relation to the site, the lower half following the street while the upper half contradicts it.

The design was ridiculed when it was first published because putting one very different building on top of another seemed absurd — yet no one objects when two very different buildings are placed side by side. Louis Kahn's Richards medical center (193, 196), for example, juxtaposes blank brick shafts with highly articulated glass and concrete towers. In this and many other examples what is admired is the contrast. But vertical stacking evidently introduces psychological problems.

However different the components of the Roman building may be, they have in common an essentially linear treatment. In the Women's Hospital in Chicago (191), a glass-walled box serves as a pedestal for a giant concrete sculpture whose flamboyant curves offer the maximum contrast, with no connecting theme whatsoever. Another kind of hybridization is achieved in the Columbus Health Center (109), where two or three different buildings appear to pass through each other without losing their identities. These variations are somewhat literal interpretations of "pluralism," and the theme is far from being exhausted.

---

190. Hardy Holzman Pfeiffer Associates. Columbus Occupational Health Center, Columbus, Ind. 1969–73

191. Bertrand Goldberg Associates. Prentice Women's Hospital and Maternity Center, and Northwestern University Psychiatric Institute, Chicago, Ill. 1970–75

192. Vincenzo, Fausto & Lucio Passarelli. Store, office, and apartment building, Rome, Italy. 1962–65

Louis Kahn

Louis Kahn (1901-1974) was a gifted and benevolent teacher whose own architecture matured relatively late in his career. At first glance its formal aspects, rarely dominated by any single preoccupation, may seem unremarkable. In its sometime pursuit of structural design his work seems "modern"; in its massing and use of materials it seems guided more by memory. Kahn opened a door to the past without engaging in historical revivalism. He seemed to have taken modern architecture apart and put it together again, making it a more subtle instrument.

The Alfred Newton Richards Medical Research and Biology Buildings were perhaps the most decisive and influential of Kahn's work in the sixties (193, 196). In them he combined laboratory towers of energetic concrete frame structure with brick shafts used for mechanical utilities. The repetition and grouping of these shafts, particularly the closely spaced units on the rear elevation, recall the castles and Romanesque churches Kahn admired so much. Something of the same embattled masonry character is also suggested in his Unitarian Church (194, 195), but here corner elements on the roof and the vertical slots are forms designed to control interior lighting.

The Library and Dining Hall at Phillips Exeter Academy are compositions of great refinement using the simplest means, primarily the proportions and spacing of rectangular openings in brick walls (200-02). The spectacular Library interior uses in a structural form the circular openings Kahn loved, but their monumental scale is concealed by bland elevations remarkable chiefly for their corner entrances.

While the Phillips Exeter buildings make no outward display of modern structural technique, and although their predominantly vertical fenestration may have Neoclassical overtones, they move toward a timelessness that seems no more attached to any previous style than to modernism. The vernacular nuances of the Dining Hall stop just short of self-conscious archaizing; that quality begins to suggest itself in the Hostels for the National Assembly at Dacca, perhaps because their size and number combine to suggest what might be a fortified town, and because the flattened brick arches used in the Phillips Exeter Dining Hall are replaced

193, 196. Louis I. Kahn. Alfred Newton Richards Medical Research and Biology Buildings, University of Pennsylvania, Philadelphia, Pa. 1957-64

194, 195. Louis I. Kahn. First Unitarian Church, Rochester, N.Y. 1959-63

by dramatic (and redundant) brick arches used both to open the buildings and to provide interior perspectives (197, 199). The Assembly Building itself (198 and p. 116) combines concrete walls with inset strips of white marble; the attached mosque juxtaposes round, square, and triangular openings in a manner at once abstract and mysterious. With these buildings, still unfinished, Kahn came closer than ever to an architecture that transcends time and place, and is yet a uniquely personal response to the circumstances that shaped it.

197, 199. Louis I. Kahn. Hostels for National Assembly, Sher-e-Banglanagar, Dacca, Bangladesh. 1962–

198. Louis I. Kahn. National Assembly Complex, Sher-e-Banglanagar, Dacca, Bangladesh. 1962–

200, 201. Louis I. Kahn. Library, Phillips Exeter Academy, Exeter, N.H. 1967-72

202. Louis I. Kahn. Dining Hall, Phillips Exeter Academy, Exeter, N.H. 1967-72

James Stirling

James Stirling's architecture, like Louis Kahn's, is remarkable for its consistency. More than other architects in the last 20 years Stirling has drawn on the industrial vernacular and, to a lesser extent, on the prewar history of modern architecture as high art.

By now the most famous, and perhaps the best, of his quasi-vernacular compositions is the Engineering Building for Leicester University (203, 206). Even after prolonged examination it looks as if it really could have been the work of engineers and other specialists, some of them manufacturers of windows and skylights. All the parts seem to have been brought together without regard for the final result, and yet the assemblage is artfully harmonious, as such exercises seldom are. Behind the fragile mask of empiricism is a hard core of poetic irrationality.

Some of the harmony derives from the repetition of angled planes. The two auditoriums cantilevered in different directions are as rational as cantilevers can be; the skylights on the low wing (206, at the far right) are quite reasonably turned 90 degrees to face north, only incidentally generating a lively perimeter detail. The awning windows on the smaller block at the left, however, and the offset columns at the base of the tower, which produce an interesting buttress detail, are explicable perhaps more readily in aesthetic than practical terms. Thus the offset columns allow an excellent opportunity to drape the glazing over the structure; the awning windows sustain the note of faceted angularity at a suitably smaller scale. A ramp, pipe railings, and mandatory funnel vary the industrial-nautical theme.

For the Engineering Building asymmetry reinforces the look of unself-conscious improvisation. It also produces a composition that is picturesque in the eighteenth-century sense of the term—and the photograph (206) is taken from the viewpoint for which the "picture" is composed. The History Faculty Building at Cambridge uses glazing details of industrial character but in a symmetrical configuration, presumably meant to suggest institutional formality (204, 205). From the outside the glazed lantern lighting the main reading room might almost suggest a nineteenth-century train shed; inside the glass follows a different contour and rides roughshod across the enclosing walls. The cascade

203, 206. James Stirling and James Gowan. Leicester University Engineering Building, Leicester, England. 1959-63

204, 205. James Stirling. Cambridge University History Faculty Building, Cambridge, England. 1964-68

of glass, in conjunction with ribbon windows interrupted by projecting bays, produces effects that are at once chaotic and delicate. Less persuasive are the inclined walls and external structural buttresses of the student residence at Oxford University (207) but the asymmetrical faceting relates the building to its river site.

A different sort of industrial vernacular is recalled by the Olivetti Training School (208-10). Wall panels of molded plastic (colored tan and pale yellow) and the finlike projections on the roof of the central block, which house movable walls, contribute to the look of an industrial appliance. Unexpectedly, the glass-roofed unit connecting the various wings reverts to the sharp facets of nineteenth-century industrial glazing techniques. Sleek opacity and brittle transparency reinforce each other's qualities. As in most of Stirling's buildings, each detail is seized upon and exploited for effects of scale. Perhaps this determination to expand, rather than reduce, the possibilities at his disposal accounts for some recent developments in his work (see p. 164).

---

207. James Stirling. The Florey Building, student residence, Queen's College, Oxford University, Oxford, England. 1966-71

208-10. James Stirling. Olivetti Training School, Haslemere, England. 1969-72

Robert Venturi

The argument stated by Robert Venturi in his book *Complexity and Contradiction in Architecture*, published by The Museum of Modern Art in 1966, claimed that modern architecture has been handicapped by a commitment to the ideas of simplicity and consistency. In their place he proposed an attitude toward architecture more consistent with life itself, namely, that we learn to live with contradictions. Moreover, where contradictions do not already exist we can invent them.

Venturi distinguishes between buildings intended to be of unique interest and those that are best treated as commonplace; in his own work he has been remarkably skillful in incorporating references to modern building styles previously noted only for their banality. Guild House and the Dixwell Fire Station (215, 212) are examples of design precariously lifted above the inept, ostensibly because the original mode is thought to have congenial associations for the occupants. The building for the Visiting Nurse Association (211) rearranges motifs from the more sophisticated reaches of modernism, but contradicts them by adding decorative moldings to frame some windows. Moldings play a more important role in the Chestnut Hill house (214), where with pitched roofs and an arched window they suggest, but only at first glance, a kind of undistinguished suburban bungalow. In more recent work like the Tucker and Brant houses (213 and p. 162) references to historic styles fall somewhere between the vernacular and High Art, the Brant house in particular moving more forthrightly toward classical design.

Venturi's work reflects the loss of faith in any single principle of integration, coupled with an insistence on recognizing possibilities modern architecture has heretofore largely excluded. His ideas and his work have influenced many younger architects, directing attention toward isolated elements of design and the sometimes rewarding associations their novel rearrangement can generate.

---

211. Venturi and Short. North Penn Visiting Nurse Association Headquarters Building, Ambler, Pa. 1960-62

212. Venturi and Rauch. Dixwell Fire Station, New Haven, Conn. 1970-74

213. Venturi and Rauch. Tucker House, Katonah, N.Y. 1974-75

214. Venturi and Rauch. Private house, Chestnut Hill, Pa. 1962-64

215. Venturi and Rauch; Cope and Lippincott. Guild House, Friends Housing for the Elderly, Philadelphia, Pa. 1960-63

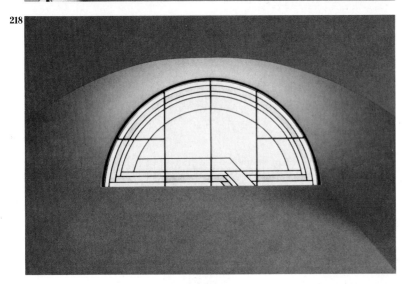

Elements: Windows

Orthodox modernism's guiding principle has been the design of structure. As the authority of that aesthetic weakened, attention returned to the design of nonstructural elements and the enhancement of their unique qualities. Doors, windows, parapets, and roofs can all be manipulated with relative ease, and the uses of the window best illustrate how a single element can eventually provide a new mode of organization.

The simplest way to enhance an opening in a wall is to use an unfamiliar shape, or a familiar one in an unexpected way, like the square window Edward Larrabee Barnes rotates 45 degrees, or his decorated half-circle set in a niche (216, 218). The revival of circular wall openings is now associated with Louis Kahn, who used them for monumental effect (see p. 104). In Japan, where they recall intimacy and tradition, Kisho Kurokawa has equipped them with rotating blinds and given them an industrial context (217, 279). The late Carlo Scarpa, on the other hand, was a most subtle master of architectural translation from the Chinese. His split-circle window for a Gavina store and his elliptical window in an Olivetti showroom are inflected by his own sense of detail, giving these Oriental motifs an Italian accent (220, 221).

These examples are confined to the wall plane; Marcel Breuer's faceted frames for his Whitney Museum of American Art project the window beyond the wall so that it seems to stare down the street (see p. 34). Breuer and others have also used the frame for an opposing effect: precast concrete panels to make "blind" window-walls of insistent and ultimately fatiguing pattern (228). Paul Rudolph's Milam house (233) used the Corbusian *brise-soleil* at a scale large enough to imply a room behind each boxlike frame, expanding this element with the same exuberance recently shown by architects borrowing from LeCorbusier's work of the twenties (see p. 44).

For vertical buildings requiring small openings, windows can be grouped in random

216. Edward Larrabee Barnes. Snell Music Building and William Moore Dietel Library, Emma Willard School, Troy, N.Y. 1964-67

217. Kisho Kurokawa Architect & Associates. Nakagin Capsule Tower hotel, Tokyo, Japan. 1970-72

218. Edward Larrabee Barnes. Cathedral of the Immaculate Conception, Burlington, Vt. 1974-76

219. Mayuimi Miyawaki. Green Box House #2, Fujisawa, Kanagawa Prefecture, Japan. 1972

220. Carlo Scarpa. Gavina Showroom, Bologna, Italy. 1960-61

221. Carlo Scarpa. Olivetti Showroom, Venice, Italy. 1957-58

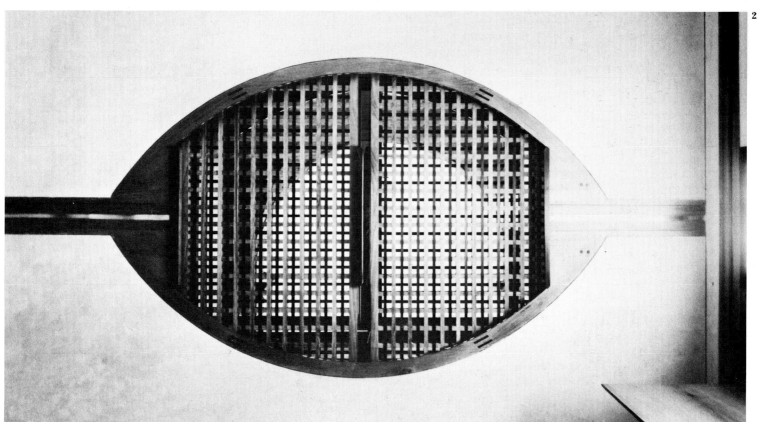

slots or evenly distributed as portholes. The slotted walls in Piero Bottoni's City Hall tilt forward at each floor, so that the inside wall surfaces can be top-lighted (225, 226). Kazuhiro Ishii combines 54 windows of assorted shapes (229); Hiromi Fujii cuts square windows into a wall to disclose another wall behind it, with more windows of different sizes revealing a third wall with still more windows (231).

222. Carson, Lundin & Shaw. Manufacturers Hanover Trust Co. Operations Center, New York, N.Y. 1966-68

223. Harry Weese & Associates. William J. Campbell Courthouse Annex, Chicago, Ill. 1972-75

224. A. C. Ledner & Associates. Joseph Curran Annex Building, National Maritime Union, New York, N.Y. 1963-66

225, 226. Piero Bottoni. City Hall of Sesto San Giovanni, Italy. 1966-70

227. John Carl Warnecke & Associates. Pacific Telephone & Telegraph Co. Equipment Building, Oakland, Calif. 1961-68

228. Marcel Breuer and Hamilton P. Smith. Becton Engineering & Applied Science Center, Yale University, New Haven, Conn. 1966-70

229. Kazuhiro Ishii. "54 Windows" house and clinic, Hiratsuka City, Kanagawa Prefecture, Japan. 1973-75

230. Louis I. Kahn. National Assembly Complex, Sher-e-Banglanagar, Dacca, Bangladesh. 1962-

231. Hiromi Fujii. Marutake Building, Saitama Prefecture, Japan. 1976

232. Takefumi Aida. Pension-style Hotel, Shiobara, Tochigi Prefecture, Japan. 1975-76

233. Paul Rudolph. Milam House, Jacksonville, Fla. 1960-62

234. I.M. Pei & Partners. Des Moines Art Center Addition, Des Moines, Iowa. 1966-68

239

Elements: Colonnade and Roof

Beginning in the late fifties many architects favored closely spaced perimeter columns and visible roofs as a means of giving some sort of dignified presence to institutional buildings. Other architects rejected these motifs because the proliferation of columns and the sometimes arbitrary development of an attic floor, in lieu of a pitched roof, suggested classical yearnings they deemed sentimental or banal. The evolution of these related motifs follows no fixed schedule, but at first their use was influenced by a certain embarrassment in recalling historical precedents. Thus Oscar Niemeyer's President's Palace in Brasilia turns an arcade upside down (235). Stood on its head it becomes a heavy base tapering upward to needle-point supports for a thin flat roof. It is set right side up again in Philip Johnson's Amon Carter Museum of Western Art, but it is rigidly encased as a frontispiece (236). In Niemeyer's Mondadori office building, 15 years later, the significant novelty is the rhythmically varied spacing of extra columns (237). The concrete structure has a conventional steel-and-glass box suspended within it.

In the early sixties the projecting attic floor with a frieze of narrow windows was combined with columns flared at the bottom and top. Because they are so thin such columns tend to look like congealed taffy that has dripped from the underside of the attic story. This effect is disliked by most architects but is often appreciated by laymen, who correctly interpret soft curves as signaling a desire to please. The undisputed masters of such beguiling effects have been Minoru Yamasaki and Edward Stone (239, 240). The latter's Beckman Auditorium is an elegant and exceptional example of the genre, being round rather than rectangular, and with its conical roof giving a graceful rather than a heavy conclusion. Nevertheless, during the sixties the heavy attic story emerged as the decisive element, as if in response to criticism that earlier versions looked flimsy. Some European observers thought the popularity of these buildings in the United States signified a new, overbearing "imperial temple" style, although Americans meant them to be dignified and only welcoming, like John Carl Warnecke's State Capitol at Honolulu (243). Here the familiar ingredients are combined with an atrium and gracefully curved outer walls rising from pools. The design not only extends the type to still larger and more important public buildings, but also has been regarded as regionally appropriate. This building type was drastically modified by Gordon Bunshaft for his Lyndon Baines Johnson Library (244). Intending monumentality (because people would enjoy it) Bunshaft discarded columns in favor of massive sloping walls and an attic floor of heroic structural dimensions. The result was seen by some not as "imperial" but as "Pharaonic" —a literary distinction prompted, perhaps, by blank walls and the unremitting use of polished travertine. Monumentality remains problematic, reactions to it being influenced by the way we regard institutions and public figures. These variations on the colonnade and attic motif, which begin with a concern for distinction and grace, move quickly toward a monumental scale disquieting to critics if not to the public. They were in part a reaction to the Brutalist style favored in Europe, but their problematic nature leaves architects still searching for a building type suitable to the grand occasion.

---

235. Oscar Niemeyer. President's Palace, Brasilia, Brazil. 1957-59

236. Philip Johnson. Amon Carter Museum of Western Art, Fort Worth, Tex. 1958-61

237. Oscar Niemeyer. Mondadori Headquarters Building, Milan, Italy. 1973-76

238. Wilson, Morris, Crain & Anderson. Heights State Bank, Houston, Tex. 1960-62

239. Minoru Yamasaki and Associates. Northwestern National Life Insurance Co., Minneapolis, Minn. 1961-64

240. Edward Durell Stone. Beckman Auditorium, California Institute of Technology, Pasadena, Calif. 1960-64

241. Minoru Yamasaki and Associates. Woodrow Wilson School of Public and International Affairs, Princeton University, Princeton, N.J. 1961-65

242. Houstoun, Albuty, Baldwin and Parish. Mutual of Omaha Office Building, Miami, Fla. 1965-68

243. John Carl Warnecke & Associates; Belt, Lemmon and Lo. Hawaii State Capitol, Honolulu, Hawaii. 1960-69

244. Skidmore, Owings & Merrill (Gordon Bunshaft); Brooks, Barr, Graeber & White. Lyndon Baines Johnson Library, University of Texas, Austin, Tex. 1968-71

240

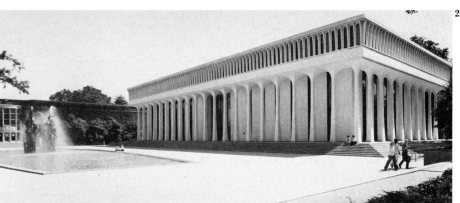
241

242

243

244

Elements: Wall into Roof

For Western architecture the roof has seldom been a decisive aesthetic element of composition. The sense of shelter has usually been conveyed by massive walls, which have also been the chief recipients of ornament and elaboration; even the Renaissance dome is a wall turned in on itself. In our great churches and palaces roofs do not overhang walls like protecting umbrellas, as they do in Oriental buildings. Modern architecture tended first to keep roofs flat, when visible, and then to eliminate visible roofs altogether. Current anxiety over restoring a visible roof to the skyscraper is somewhat belated, since experiments with the relation of wall to roof have been going on for over 20 years. Not surprisingly, some of the most original are by Japanese architects, for whom a Western-inspired wall-and-flat-roof architecture represents a drastic break with their own tradition. Efforts to preserve a visible roofline usually take their cue from the nature and material of the wall itself. Thus, a concrete office building in Tokyo is given a steeply pitched concrete roof (245); a glass department store in Stockholm has a glass mansard (247). Both buildings remain "modern" by subordinating the roof to the wall. More drastic are those transformations whereby the wall as a vertical element is made to disappear entirely (pp. 122–23), by being absorbed into a roof which then seems to become the whole building, like an A-frame vacation house or, as the late Sibyl Moholy-Nagy once described it, like an attic without a house. In the countryside such compositions make large buildings seem more at ease, as if they were hills; in cities they tend to take on the scale and proportions of pyramids, like Edgar Fonseca's unfinished cathedral in Rio de Janeiro (250).

245. Takenaka Komuten Co. Ltd. Lapin d'Or Building, Tokyo, Japan. 1969-71

246. Rinaldo Olivieri. "La Pyramide" commercial center. Abidjan, Ivory Coast. 1968-73

247. Erik & Tore Ahlsén. PUB Department Store, Stockholm, Sweden. 1956-60

248. Sachio Otani. Kyoto International Conference Hall, Kyoto, Japan. 1964-66

249. Hermann Schroder, Roland Frey, Peter Faller, Claus Schmidt. "Housing Hill," Marl, Germany. 1965-68

250. Edgar Fonseca. Cathedral of St. Sebastian, Rio de Janeiro, Brazil. 1964-76

251. Bert Allemann, Hans Stuenzi. Weekend house, Engelberg, Switzerland. 1966-67

252. Jacques Labro; Orzoni & Roques. Hotel des Dromonts, Avoriaz, France. 1964-67

253. Justus Dahinden. Ferro-Haus office and residential building, Zurich, Switzerland. 1968-70

251

252

253

254

255

256

Elements: Parapets

Buildings designed in the Wrightian manner with cantilevered terraces that seem to float in the air have the effect of "demolishing the box," as Wright put it, because their varying projections obscure the continuity of the wall plane. For large buildings this requires more cantilevered terraces than is practical: nevertheless, the terrace and its parapet, and the emphasis on horizontality they generate, have never been altogether abandoned. It should also be noted that of all modern motifs this one is the most incompatible with historic Western styles, and hence the most disruptive to the urban scene. Among the few building types that readily lend themselves to Wright's spatial conception is the open garage and its spiral access ramp. The group of four ramps at Seattle's airport garage suggests a collection of coil springs and may well be the most exuberant of its kind (256).

Luigi Moretti's apartment house in Rome is a rectangular block from which semicircular balconies are cantilevered at slightly different positions on each floor, giving the building the animation of a flowering plant (257). Ulrich Franzen's Alley Theater in Houston uses parapets in gentle arcs, against a massive blank-walled backdrop (258). On very large buildings the consistent use of such terraces generates effects that seem almost geological, like Michel Marot and André Minangoy's curved apartment blocks in France resembling terraced mountains (261); or obsessive, like the angled terraces in William Morgan's Florida apartment house where outside stairs add optical distortion (262). Enrico Taglietti's motel in Australia has rectilinear terraces cantilevered at all sides, but where the parapets meet the corner is chamfered and extended visually with a projecting beam like a downspout (263). The sloping corners emphatically terminate the horizontals and evoke Oriental pagodas, because each floor can be read equally well as a roof.

---

254. Frank Lloyd Wright. Fallingwater, house for Edgar Kaufmann, Bear Run, Pa. 1935-37

255. Paul Rudolph. New Haven Parking Garage, New Haven, Conn. 1959-63

256, 259. The Richardson Associates. Sea-Tac International Airport Parking Terminal, Seattle, Wash. 1969-72

257. Luigi W. Moretti. "San Maurizio" condominium apartment block, Rome, Italy. 1962-65

258. Ulrich Franzen & Associates. Alley Theater, Houston, Tex. 1966-68

260. Luigi W. Moretti; Fischer-Elmore Associated Architects. The Watergate Apartments, Washington, D.C. 1961-64/70

261. Michel Marot & André Minangoy. Marina Baie des Anges, Villeneuve Loubet, France. 1968-78

262. William Morgan Architects. Pyramid Condominium Apartments, Ocean City, Md. 1971-75

263. Enrico Taglietti. Town House Motel, Wagga-Wagga, N.S.W., Australia. 1962-64

Elements: Earth

By the late fifties the sheer proliferation of new buildings, good and bad, provoked questions about why so many of them had to be visible, especially when their utilitarian nature did not require architectural "statements." Why, for example, could not a warehouse be at least partly underground, with its roof used for gardens and terraces? The first efforts to design such structures were prompted by aesthetics, rather than the more recent concern with thermal efficiency. The most important was the desire to avoid the destruction of a site.

For Kevin Roche's Oakland Museum, the only available site was a small park (264). Roche successfully handled this large building as a kind of landscape design—a terracing of the park that both completes and improves it. Bernard Zehrfuss's UNESCO Annex in Paris is completely underground, its offices opening on sunken courtyards to avoid further obstructing a heavily built-up site (265). Universities have been interested in this approach when a new building, usually a library, might damage a campus layout. The sequestered garden, visible from above, in Rhone and Iredale's underground library for a university is the only "disruption" the new addition causes (266). Not all such buildings strive for total invisibility, nor are they always underground: Ove Arup's office building unexpectedly combines a densely planted roofscape with the hard-edge geometry of steel-cage construction (267).

Sloping sites lend themselves to hemicycle plans in which the roof can sometimes be used as a garden promenade, as with Olivetti's staff housing at Ivrea (268); or the roof may be concealed under earth to leave visible only a curved wall, like Hellmuth, Obata and Kassabaum's fire station resembling a Chinese tomb (269). All these solutions retain elements of conventional architecture, but it is also possible to design earth structures naturalistically rounded like artificial mountains or geometrically trimmed like mastabas. Geometric solutions

---

264. Kevin Roche John Dinkeloo and Associates. Oakland Museum, Oakland, Calif. 1962-68

265. Bernard Zehrfuss. UNESCO Annex, Paris, France. 1962-65

266. Rhone & Iredale Architects. Sedgewick Library, University of British Columbia, Vancouver, Canada. 1969-72

267. Arup Associates. Wiggins Teape office building, Basingstoke, Hampshire, England. 1973-76

268. Roberto Gabetti & Almaro Isola. Olivetti housing, Ivrea, Italy. 1967-68

269. Hellmuth, Obata & Kassabaum. St. Louis Fire Alarm Headquarters Building, St. Louis, Mo. 1957-59

seem more convincing architecturally when their rooms open onto interior courtyards. Naturalistic design is difficult to relate consistently to such mundane features as doors and windows, but can lead to entertaining variations like the openings of William Morgan's Dunehouse (273).

270. Timo & Tuomo Suomalainen. Temppeliaukio Church, Helsinki, Finland. 1960-69

271. William Morgan Architects. Hilltop Residence, Central Florida. 1972-75

272. Takefumi Aida. PL Institute Kindergarten, Osaka, Japan. 1972-73

273. William Morgan Architects. Dunehouse, Atlantic Beach, Fla. 1974-75

274

275

276

277

Elements: Detachable Parts

Related to the preoccupation with mega-structure (see p. 26) is the use of prefabricated components clipped on to a supporting structure. Such components fragment architecture quite literally into elements whose manner of use is intended to imply change. The most dramatic and fully realized example is Kisho Kurokawa's Nakagin Capsule Tower, a hotel in which each room is a small steel box equipped with bed, bath, desk, and circular window, the latter said to remind Japanese of bird houses (278, 279). Flexibility is the alleged practical advantage of such systems: in theory the attachments might be pulled off and reassembled in some other arrangement, although it is hard to think why. Most applications fall short of Kurokawa's complete boxes, settling instead for large sections of wall shaped to make sculptural projections. Yoji Watanabe uses large aluminum plates, together with a penthouse like a gunturret, to suggest a battleship (276). Fertility, rather than warfare, is evoked by the planters hung from Gérard Grandval's apartment house (274) like the breasts on the ancient Greek representations of Artemis (although some observers are reminded of lifeboats). The point of such strenuous efforts, notwithstanding their rationalizations, is that uninteresting building programs may be enlivened by novel combinations of a single unit of design. Some are more persuasive than others.

---

274. Gérard Grandval. "Les Choux" housing, Créteil, France. 1970-74

275. Tatsuhiko Nakajima & Urban Science Laboratory. Youth Castle in Kibogaoka Park, Shiga Prefecture, Japan. 1968-72

276. Yoji Watanabe. Sky Building No. 3 apartment house, Shinjuku-ku, Tokyo, Japan. 1967-70

277. Andrault & Parat. Housing at Ste. Geneviève des Bois, France. 1968

278, 279. Kisho Kurokawa Architect & Associates. Nakagin Capsule Tower Hotel, Tokyo, Japan. 1970-72

Vernacular: Roofs

Isolating the elements of design does more than weaken those systematically "purist" conceptions of architecture derived from engineering and abstract art. It opens architecture to the modest inventions characteristic of vernacular building, and vernacular building opens architecure to history. Even the cheapest house, for instance, can have at least one unusual window, or a recognizable roof. Windows are relatively easy to design; roofs are more difficult and costly, but it is the shape of a roof that most clearly signals the undogmatic sympathy with the past implied by the words "vernacular" and "regional."

For modern architecture the relation of wall to roof is ambiguous and often problematic (see pp. 120–23). "Roofline," as we habitually understand it, refers to the top of a wall seen against the sky, rather than to the three-dimensional roof itself. Varying the profile of the wall, as Edward Larrabee Barnes did in his New England school buildings, may or may not evoke regional history through the transformation of details: in these examples the pitch of a roofline is determined by the rotation of a square window (282, 283). Their geometrically unalterable relation establishes a kind of order; that Barnes intends clear order, rather than the flexible profusion of the picturesque, is equally apparent in the systematic layout of his Haystack Mountain School (280). And yet picturesqueness too may be generated quite systematically, as it is in Marot Tremblot's row houses at Amboise, where an increase of one story for each unit makes the gable ends of their pitched roofs read as dominant elevations (284).

Japan's contribution to modern architecture during the last 20 years is spectacular and well known, but critical appreciation rarely acknowledges the continuing vitality of the Japanese classical tradition, in which the roof is preeminent. It is a tradition that accommodates lyric spontaneity, as in Junzo Yoshimura's teahouse (286); or formal dignity, as in Isoya Yoshida's Matsushita Pavilion (285). Pitch and relation to walls and columns provide the most direct means of

280. Edward Larrabee Barnes. Haystack Mountain School of Arts & Crafts, Deer Isle, Maine. 1959-60

281. Abe Bonnema. Municipal Social Service Building with apartments, Leeuwarden, Holland. 1972-75

282. Edward Larrabee Barnes. Boys' Dormitories and Masters' Housing, St. Paul's School, Concord, N.H. 1960-61

283. Edward Larrabee Barnes. Snell Music Building and William Moore Dietel Library, Emma Willard School, Troy, N.Y. 1964-67

284. M.T.A. Marot Tremblot. La Verrerie Housing, Amboise, France. 1970-74

varying roof designs; materials and texture, and the relation of one roof to another, introduce useful complications. Visible roofs as the determinant of form have been largely neglected by modern architecture because they have been thought unsuitable, or impractical, for buildings larger than houses. But the evolution of vernacular architecture has addressed itself to just that problem. In the last 20 years the scope of roof design has been extended until it can deal with buildings of almost any scale, including the skyscraper. Among the first and most interesting attemps to organize groups of large buildings as roof architecture was Ernest J. Kump's campus for Foothill College in California (290). The silhouette, varied in places, is a hipped roof with a boxlike crown. The crown replaces a ridge and is useful for housing mechanical equipment. It suggest, among other precedents, the Japanese *irimoya* roof (a hipped roof modified by the insertion of a small gable on the narrow ends) without using any specifically Japanese details. Variations on Kump's design are now familiar across the United States; the practical advantages of the crown make this kind of roof economical for commercial buildings.

---

285. Isoya Yoshida. Matsushita Pavilion, Expo '70, Osaka, Japan. 1970

286. Junzo Yoshimura. Japanese teahouse, Rockefeller Estate, Tarrytown, N.Y. 1960–63

287. Hiroyuki Iwamoto. Yamamoto House, Ashiya, Japan. 1963-65

288. Skidmore, Owings & Merrill. Chapel, Carmel Valley Manor Retirement Village, Carmel, Calif. 1961-63

289. Huygens and Tappé, Inc. Private house, Connecticut. 1969–72

290. Ernest J. Kump Associates; Masten & Hurd. Foothill College, Los Altos, Calif. 1958-61

A church, an office, a library, and two houses illustrate some problems and advantages of roof design which does not automatically communicate the nature of a building. The church might be an unusually elegant market hall; the office might be a house. Walter Netsch's library is particularly interesting in its use of an overhanging roof as if it were a starched handkerchief draped over the walls. The roof design of Peter Rose's ski lodge differs from the others in that it is used to generate a flat facade: pitched roofs on the sides help to make the main elevation seem like a section, as if the building had been cut in half and only partially walled in.

291. Robert Maguire & Keith Murray. All Saints' Church, Crewe, England. 1962-66

292. The Kling Partnership. Cargill Office Center, Minnetonka, Minn. 1974-77

293. Norman Jaffe. Weekend house, Montauk, N.Y. 1974-76

294. Skidmore, Owings & Merrill (Walter Netsch). Louis Jefferson Long Library, Wells College, Aurora, N.Y. 1966-68

295. James Volney Righter. Osborn House, New York State. 1972-73

296. Peter Rose, Peter Lanken, James Righter. "Pavillon 70" ski-area base building, St. Sauveur, Quebec, Canada. 1976-77

Vernacular roof design shades into formal quotations from historic styles. In the early sixties such allusions were construed as a failure to toe the line of serious modernism, either through weakness or frivolity. Sometimes the allusions are made almost imperceptibly; sometimes with deliberate and clear intent; sometimes with wrenching violence. Richard Snibbe's elegant Tennis Pavilion at Princeton echoes Georgian chinoiserie with a "pagoda" roof and bracketed columns of toothpick delicacy (297). The eight shallow domes of Philip Johnson's Dumbarton Oaks museum are carried on massive columns and generate the undulating elevations associated with Hellenistic and Baroque architecture (299). But the building's echoes are Neoclassic. Its allusions are not attributable to any single element, unlike those of the London Central Mosque where removal of the minaret and pointed dome would restore the building to unremarkable modernism (298). Johnson's undulating wood dome with no building under it (called the Roofless Church, 300) stands in a walled garden and is more complicated still: its formality evokes a culture that cannot quite be identified—is it Hindu, with shingles? The overtones produced by these buildings summon up the past; it is also possible to use the past to suggest the future, or at least a fictional anticipation of it. The zooming roof of the Reiyukai Shakaden, a Buddhist temple in Tokyo, appears to have been built of layers thicker than any known tile or wood shingle; its version of supporting brackets is so extensive it almost obliterates the rest of the building, like the monumental stair that fills the courtyard (301). This building is a vernacular equivalent to the science-fiction fantasies of plug-in architecture (p. 132); like them it uses the "styling" of product design to transform not technology but a remembered craftsmanship.

297. Ballard, Todd & Snibbe. Tennis Pavilion, Princeton University, Princeton, N.J. 1960-61

298. Frederick Gibberd & Partners. London Central Mosque, London, England. 1969–77

299. Philip Johnson. Museum for Pre-Columbian Art, Dumbarton Oaks, Washington, D.C. 1961-63

300. Philip Johnson. Roofless Church, New Harmony, Ind. 1958-60

301. Takenaka Komuten Co. Ltd. Reiyukai Shakaden Temple, Tokyo, Japan. 1972-75

Vernacular: Roofs and Walls

The Matthew, Johnson-Marshall Hillingdon Civic Centre houses government agencies for a variety of social services. Because it is much visited by the local community, the architects were concerned with how the building would be perceived. It owes its intricacy not to any inherent complexity of accommodation, but rather to the architects' decision to avoid a monolithic, impersonal scale associated with bureaucracy. The volume is divided into increments small enough to be grasped by the eye but sufficiently varied to hold its attention. The eye comes to rest on clusters of windows and roofs combined to make units like small houses, which the imagination fills with human beings (presumably friendly). The reduction in scale is reinforced by brick, shingle roofs, and decorative detail. The internal planning is perhaps too complicated, and some of the external angles are awkward; but the amiable intention is quite clear. Something of the kind might have been achieved with a less pointed evocation of Victorian busyness, but that characteristic sets the building in its context.

Hillingdon is too artful to be taken as vernacular work, yet that seems as much its character as not. A similar uncertainty occurs, at least for the observer, with Shizutaro Urabe's Civic Center at Kurashiki. Its irregu-

302, 304. Robert Matthew, Johnson-Marshall & Partners. Hillingdon Civic Centre offices, Uxbridge, London, England. 1971-76

303. Shizutaro Urabe. Kurashiki Civic Center, Kurashiki, Okayama Prefecture, Japan. 1970-72

lar shed roofs imply that their angles were improvised rather than composed. The blank wall is decorated with designs reminiscent of those found on old warehouses and other folk architecture, and in that context the building conveys a vernacular informality. In England this middle ground between high art and the vernacular has been explored with great success. Some of the most persuasive work in this manner seems prompted by survivals from the medieval past: stone walls whose roofs have vanished, castles, barns. The house at Shipton-under-Wychwood consists of five separate small buildings grouped around a pond—some of the stone walls rise from the water. Each roof is pitched at a slightly different angle and reinforces the perspectives set up by the casual grouping of walls. The Theological College at Chichester uses massive concrete lintels to carry its brick walls, some of which are offset to allow for glass toplights. Perhaps it is the brick that rescues this building from Brutalism of the proletarian stained-concrete variety; here the blocklike forms evoke Cistercian austerities—and perhaps the excitement of defense against armed attack.

305. Roy Stout and Patrick Litchfield. Private house, Shipton-under-Wychwood, England. 1961-64

306. Ahrends Burton & Koralek. Residential building, Chichester Theological College, Chichester, England. 1962-68

307. Edward Cullinan with Julian Bicknell and Julyan Wickham. Centre for Advanced Study in the Developmental Sciences, Minster Lovell, England. 1965-69

305

Vernacular: Instant Village

Some part of the success English architects have had with what looks like a vernacular may be due to experience in preserving and adding to the real thing. The Millburngate Shopping Centre in Durham (opposite the Cathedral) uses brick and Welsh slate to blend with other buildings so thoroughly it can barely be distinguished from its surroundings. That is a rare circumstance in which accommodation to existing scales and materials is imposed. Rarer still is the effort to transform a modern theme associated with megastructure, or other versions of the gargantuan, into something rich with the local scale and incident of the picturesque, as Ralph Erskine has done with his Byker housing at Newcastle-upon-Tyne. Timber, brick, concrete, the changing roofline, and the cantilevered balconies, some of them with arbors or shed roofs, make this immense work look as if people had been improvising lean-tos against a stretch of the Roman wall.

Nothing quite comparable is to be found in the United States; our versions of the instant

---

308. Building Design Partnership. Millburngate Shopping Centre, Durham City, England. 1972-76

309, 311. Ralph Erskines Arkitektkontor AB. Byker Redevelopment housing, Newcastle-upon-Tyne, England. 1969-

310. Moore, Lyndon, Turnbull, Whitaker. Sea Ranch Condominium vacation houses, Sonoma County, Calif. 1963-65

312

village clearly rejoice in the grouping of separate buildings. Charles Moore's Sea Ranch houses (310) were recognized, as soon as they were built, as epitomizing the American response to preserving the environment, to community with privacy, and to the idea of the good but simple life. Simplicity here borders on the earnestly primitive, redeemed by a certain tongue-in-cheek humor (qualities to which students may have been responding when they dubbed the style "mine-shaft modern"). Other American versions range from holiday resorts comprising dozens of buildings (312) to school blocks made to look like dozens of buildings (313). A hybrid, combining the stepped roofs of small houses in one continuous stretch, is Marot and Tremblot's row housing in Amboise (315 and p. 135).

312. Killingsworth, Brady & Associates. Elkhorn Vacation Condominiums and Village Center, Sun Valley, Idaho. 1971-73

313. Associated Architects of Colorado, William C. Muchow/Partner in Charge. Engineering Sciences Center, University of Colorado, Boulder, Colo. 1963-65

314. Ernest J. Kump Associates; Berger-Kelley-Unteed-Scaggs & Associates. Parkland College, Champaign, Ill. 1969-73

315. M.T.A. Marot Tremblot. La Verrerie Housing, Amboise, France. 1970-74

313

314

315

The goal of owning a private house remains the undoubted preference of most Americans. Modern houses are now provided by some developers and their architects with a skill that has improved conspicuously. In large part this improvement is due to the imposition of marketing techniques on architecture. The size, shapes, materials, and details, and the amount of space between houses, are determined by analysis of consumer expectations, graded according to differences in income level. Once he knows your income the developer can predict your taste. Everything is factored into the equation, including art and sentiment, and the result is better than most architectural critics are prepared to believe. The process arouses the same critical hostility as the manipulativeness of Disneyland; yet the "product" pleases people — many of them intelligent — and seems to achieve systematically what elsewhere is the occasional result of inspiration or exceptional talent. Among the most successful practitioners of this specialty are Robert Fisher and Rodney Friedman. In more than 20 communities they have evolved efficient, comfortable, attractive houses of vernacular character, enlivened by "features" cheerfully borrowed from wherever they come. This kind of architecture lacks only an intellectual pedigree to make it eligible for academic disputes. It is a defect that can be remedied by pointing out that Fisher and Friedman, like many others, have for some time been practicing what Venturi preaches.

316. Bull Field Volkmann Stockwell. Venetian Gardens houses, Stockton, Calif. 1974-77

317. Fisher-Friedman Associates. Ethan's Glen townhouses, Houston, Tex. 1972-76

318. Fisher-Friedman Associates. Mariner's Square apartments, Newport Beach, Calif. 1968-69

319, 320. Fisher-Friedman Associates. The Islands condominiums, Foster City, Calif. 1972-76

318

319

32

Vernacular: Details and Decor

Many motifs that are now part of a worldwide common language have their origin in vernacular solutions to practical problems, and for modern architecture the Japanese tradition has been a particularly rich source. It still is for the Japanese. Hiroshi Hara's small house (323), with barely more than one room to each of its three floors, adapts the formal *shoin* style, where one might have expected variations on the informal *sukiya* (teahouse) style. Hara has kept most of the familiar elements but transformed them by intensifying differences between light and dark: the black-lacquered woodwork produces vibrating contrasts where the traditional style would have ignored or minimized them. The X pattern on the balcony railing, while not unknown to the Japanese tradition, in this context looks Roman.

A counterpart to the luminous paper screens of Japanese architecture is used in William Wurster's San Francisco townhouse, where translucent glass walls enclose a garden (321). The grid pattern modifies Japanese usage by stressing the vertical; part of the wall curves around a stair; and the structure is so delicate that the columns can scarcely be distinguished from the glass frames. Harry Weese's Engineering Center, Stanford University (322), is a five-story timber-frame structure. Its upper floors are walled with narrow windows protected by sliding shutters. This kind of shutter is Western; the external storage box it slides into is Japanese. Red tile roofs and the abrupt change of scale from upper to lower stories also help to mingle the associations generated by each element.

Here the design process is perceived as skillful juxtaposition and modification, not as the quoting of established sources usually dismissed as eclecticism. That kind of quotation has been more acceptable to the modern temperament when confined to transient decor: the stage-setting of a restaurant or a showroom, for example, or the interiors of a house. Alexander Girard's Western (saloon) decor (327) made use of this exemption from orthodoxy in 1958, well before the desire to do so became widespread. By the early sixties

---

321. Wurster, Bernardi and Emmons Inc. Spreckels House, San Francisco, Calif. 1956-62

322. Harry Weese & Associates. Frederic Emmons Terman Engineering Center, Stanford University, Palo Alto, Calif. 1974-77

323. Hiroshi Hara & Atelier. Kudoh summer house, Karuizawa, Nagano Prefecture, Japan. 1976

324. David Roberts & Geoffrey Clarke. Wolfson Court, Girton College, Cambridge University, Cambridge, England. 1968-71

Charles Moore's Tuscan columns, making two aedicules in the single room of his small house (328), subtly altered the process: they are not necessarily a joke. By 1972 Reichlin and Reinhart's "Palladian" house (329 and p. 162) addresses history without so much as a smile. Something of the sort occurs also with quotations from the history of modernism: Giulio Savio's interiors (325, 326) amalgamate elements from Mackintosh and Godwin, de Stijl, Japan, the Renaissance, and contemporary graphic design. The method requires wit; the result is solemn.

325, 326. Giulio, Savio,. Remodelled condominiums in Palazzo Gaetani Lovatelli, Rome, Italy. 1968-70

327. Alexander Girard. Herman Miller Showroom, San Francisco, Calif. 1957-58

328. Charles W. Moore. Architect's house, Orinda, Calif. 1961-62

329. Bruno Reichlin and Fabio Reinhart. Tonini House, Torricella, Ticino, Switzerland. 1972-74

327

328

326

329

Fragments: The Usable Past

Vernacular architecture is often funny because of its "errors": carpenter's Gothic, for example, or provincial combinations of Greek and Roman details. Collage and assemblage have brought sophisticated method to the production of the improbable. Carlo Scarpa's storefront for Olivetti, incorporating an existing facade, exhibits the sensibilities of a painter as much as those of an architect. His added fragments realign and absorb those he has found: it is impossible to say what "style" this work represents, yet it is all style. Kimio Yokoyama intends quite the opposite effect: the Doric columns at the entrance to his museum look as if they might have been brought back from a European tour and reassembled the wrong way—that being the point for a museum. The taste for fragments leads to their being invented, as with the fluted walls and broken cornices of Marco Bardeschi's vaguely Neo-Liberty house or the facade like an unfinished jigsaw puzzle of scrambled moldings on Vittorio Mazzucconi's office building in Paris.

---

330. Carlo Scarpa. Olivetti Showroom, Venice, Italy. 1957-58

331, 332. Marco Dezzi Bardeschi. Private house, Florence, Italy. 1962-63

333. Kimio Yokoyama. Fuji Art Museum, Shizuoka Prefecture, Japan. 1971-73

334. Vittorio Mazzucconi. Matignon Building, Paris, France. 1973-76

Historicizing

Conscious flirtation with history had begun during the fifties, but at first the selection of sources was limited by the fear of eclecticism. References to historic styles were acceptable when they could be construed as by-products of objective, rationalist decisions, preferably with some functional value; the architect could not be blamed for historicizing if the result happened to remind one of Gothic tracery (335). The round arch of Mediterranean history had already been absorbed into the modern canon through the work of Le Corbusier; the pointed arch, which might well have been equated with the radicalism of Gothic structure so congenial to modern theory, was in practice limited to spans clearly too small to have structural validity (336). They were too obviously a pretext for achieving an effect of delicacy. The effect was dismissed along with the means. When the effect is more rugged, as it has been in recent work by Western architects in the Middle East (337), it can now be justified on cultural as well as structural

grounds. This produces the anomaly of Western architects rejecting the history of their own culture, but exporting paraphrases of other cultures to peoples who began by wanting the alien style of Western technological modernism — and now are not sure what they want. Twenty years after they were designed, Minoru Yamasaki's buildings for Wayne State University in Detroit seem compatible with the present surge of nationalist feeling in Iran, but in 1960 sophisticated Iranian opinion would have rejected them as patronizing.

335. Paul Rudolph; Anderson, Beckwith & Haible. Mary Cooper Jewett Arts Center, Wellesley College, Wellesley, Mass. 1955-58

336. Minoru Yamasaki and Associates. College of Education Building, Wayne State University, Detroit, Mich. 1956-59

337. Caudill Rowlett Scott, Charles E. Lawrence, Principal Architectural Designer. University of Petroleum and Minerals, Dhahran, Saudi Arabia. 1966-71/

The modern building type considered least vulnerable to historicizing has been the skyscraper, but it too has been subject to reappraisal. The multiuse program of the Torre Velasca in Milan called for offices below and apartments at the top third of the tower. When Belgiojoso, Peresutti and Rogers began to design it in 1957, their first response was to differentiate the two functions by cantilevering the upper floors beyond the structural cage and making the fenestration more delicate (338). By the time they finished in 1960 they had rejected this design in favor of a uniform pattern of conventional windows, a projecting upper block supported by four-story-high ribs, and a hipped roof surmounted by a boxlike crown (339). The justification was that this silhouette was more compatible with the character of the city: it looked "regional" in that it reminded observers of medieval fortifications, among other things, but for the same reason it was widely condemned by architects and critics. Importantly, the historical associations were defended as utilitarian and *vernacular*, and hence without frivolity or moral taint. Almost 20 years later it is the pseudovernacular aspect that might seem frivolous. Recent efforts, like the Bank of America's pipe-organ clusters of San Francisco bay windows (341), seem more relaxed — so much so that the building has escaped condemnation for its vernacular historicizing. (But that is also because everyone likes bay windows.) Functional justifications and forms that avoid direct historical references are still the easiest to accept: the Crédit Lyonnais office-hotel tower in Lyons (340) has a pyramidal roof whose silhouette is compatible with older buildings; it is transparent and lights an interior court (see p. 99). What remains shocking — this year — is a visible roof that refers to a specific historical style and has no function at all, except to be seen. Philip Johnson's tower for AT&T in New York (342) provides this visibility with a broken pediment of Neoclassical provenance, and offers similar but less flamboyantly historical references at street level. Ten years from now it will be interesting to see if this building seems only a straightforward but modest step in the process of retrieving the past, and not so decisive a rejection of modernism.

338, 339. Belgiojoso, Peresutti, Rogers. Torre Velasca, Milan, Italy. 1957-60

340. Cossutta & Associates. Crédit Lyonnais Tower, Lyons, France. 1972-74

341. Wurster, Bernardi and Emmons Inc.; Skidmore, Owings & Merrill. Bank of America World Headquarters, San Francisco, Calif. 1965-69

342. Johnson/Burgee; Simmons Architects. AT&T Corporate Headquarters (model), New York, N.Y. 1977-

Although it aroused no great controversy at the time, a classicizing predecessor to Philip Johnson's AT&T building was his addition to the Boston Public Library (343). Designed in 1965 and completed in 1973, its plan of nine square bays with massive piers at each corner echoes his 1963 Dumbarton Oaks museum (p. 140). The arches are not structural — floors are suspended from roof trusses — and the scale of the component parts recalls the giantism associated with Ledoux and Boullée (those eighteenth-century masters of stripped classical form whose works may yet become a primary source of inspiration for modern architecture in its present historicizing mood). A centralized, nine-bay plan is also used by Reichlin and Reinhart in their small house (344 and p. 155). But where Johnson's Library addition makes its classical forms look structural, and to that extent "modern," the Palladian formality of the Reichlin house is modernized by eroded corners and a "symbolic" arch.

Comparable manipulations occur in the treatment of moldings, and the round window that breaks into them, in Venturi and Rauch's Brant House (345, pictured in construction). Here Venturi's modification of classical motifs is without obvious irony. The forms are strong enough to survive his treatment of them; at any rate they read as if the observer is meant to find them beautiful before noticing anything clever.

Charles Moore's Piazza d'Italia in New Orleans (347) recalls collections of models and casts seen in nineteenth-century photographs of the Ecole des Beaux Arts. Its pieces of classical colonnade, polished aluminum columns and capitals, neon lights, and a pool shaped like a map of Italy, together with relief sculptures of the architect spouting water, combine to advance the possibilities of classicizing under cover of good clean fun. Moore's memorial is without the slightly sinister overtones of Ricardo Bofill's Monument to Catalonia, a walled plaza on the summit of a pyramidal slope (346). Twisted piers of brick and ghosts of classical details contribute to the air of ceremony for something no one can quite remember. It is a quality or a

343. Johnson/Burgee; Architects Design Group. Boston Public Library Addition, Boston, Mass. 1965-73

344. Bruno Reichlin and Fabio Reinhart. Tonini House, Torricella, Ticino, Switzerland. 1972-74

345. Venturi and Rauch. Brant House, Bermuda. 1975-78

346. Ricardo Bofill; Taller de Arquitectura. Le Perthus, Monument to Catalonia, French-Spanish border. 1974-76

347. Urban Innovations Group, Charles Moore; August Perez & Associates. St. Joseph's Fountain in Piazza d'Italia, New Orleans, La. 1974-78

tone that apparently interests several architects, as can be inferred from the arches and columns of Michael Graves's Fargo-Moorhead Cultural Center (349, detail) and the serpentine barrel vault of Arata Isozaki's Fujimi Country Club (350). Graves places an exhibition hall on a bridge to join two towns separated by a river: hence the symbolism of the parallel arches slightly out of alignment.

Two buildings scheduled for construction in 1979 are of particular interest for the character of their historicizing. James Stirling's addition to Stuttgart's State Galleries (348) will have a pedestrian passage traversing the site, without interfering with museum functions (the model shows the existing building at the bottom left). This is provided by a walkway that cuts across a gallery roof and breaks into a circular, walled sculpture court, affording pedestrians a view down into it but no access. The walkway exits at the opposite side to a ramp and the plaza below. Recollections of the round, moated library of

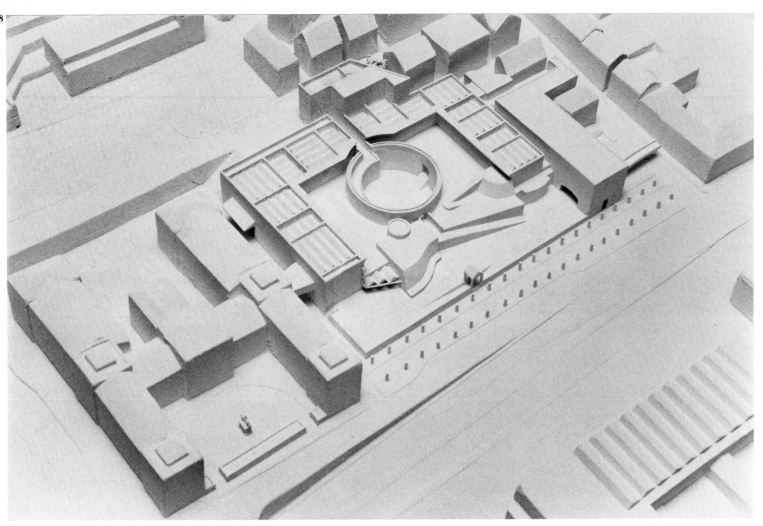

349

350

Hadrian's Villa, together with a monumental ramp, distance this work from Stirling's earlier industrial style. Kevin Roche's suburban headquarters (351, 352) for a large American corporation is U-shaped in plan, the central wing being dominated by a rotunda, and the arms reaching out to embrace a lake crossed by a causeway. This classical plan is without classicizing detail. The walls are to be of white clapboard siding—aluminum, not wood—introducing a cheerful domestic note in what is in other respects a Beaux Arts palace.

348. James Stirling and Partner. State Galleries (model), Stuttgart, Germany. 1977–

349. Michael Graves. Fargo-Moorhead Cultural Center (detail), Fargo, N. Dak., and Moorhead, Minn. 1977-78

350. Arata Isozaki. Fujimi Country Club, Oita City, Japan. 1973-74

351, 352. Kevin Roche John Dinkeloo & Associates. Corporate headquarters (model), New York State. 1977–

List of Architects

In the list that follows the numbers refer to pages on which works are illustrated.

Photo Sources

Photographs of buildings reproduced were, in most cases, provided by the architect or owner, to whom we are most grateful. The following list, keyed to page number for the Introduction and to photograph number for the balance of the book, applies to photographs for which a separate acknowledgment is due:

Introduction:
AB Vägforbattringar, Foto Manne Lind, Sweden, 4 top
©Architectural Review, London, England, (Colin Partridge and Jeffrey Taylor), 11 top
Martin Charles, Twickenham, England, 15 top
Frank H. Conant, M.I.T. Photographic Service, Cambridge, Mass., 13 top
©Walt Disney Productions, 6
Nassos Hadjopoulos, 10 top
Alex Langley for Time, New York, 14 bottom
Lautman Photography, Washington, D.C., 11 third and fourth
H. Madensky, Vienna, Austria, 11 second
William Maris, New York, N.Y., 15 bottom
Stewart's Commercial Photographers, Colorado Springs, Colo., 14 top
Ezra Stoller, Mamaroneck, N.Y., 10 bottom and 13 bottom
© Ulster Museum, Belfast, Northern Ireland, 15 center

Plates:
Agapa, Photo Ciné Publicité, 246
Erol Akyavas, 34
Chalmer Alexander, 105
Gil Amiaga, New York, N.Y., 11
©Architectural Review, London, England, 307, 309, 311
David Atkin (Dev Reemer), London, England, 298
Gaio Bacci, Rome, Italy, 35
Morley Baer, Monterey, Calif., 30, 227, 243, 288, 310, 313, 328
G. Berengo Gardin, 268
Roger Bester, New York, N.Y., 250
Hans L. Blohm, Ottawa, Canada, 189
Branko Lenart, Glaserwegs, Austria, 78
Brecht-Einzig, London, England, 2, 5, 204-07, 209, 210, 267, 305, 324
Bureau d'Informations d'Avoriaz, Paris, France, 252
Orlando R. Cabanban, Chicago, Ill., 93
Ludovico Canali, Rome, Italy, 192
M. Capapetian, London, England, 203
Casali, 220

F. Catala-Roca, Barcelona, Spain, 136
Martin Charles, Twickenham, England, 101, 103
Louis Checkman, Jersey City, N.J., 170, 342
Tom Crane, Bryn Mawr, Pa., 213
Creative Photographic Service, Jacksonville, Fla., 271, 273
George Cserna, New York, N.Y., 29, 83, 155, 297
Deutsche Luftbild, Hamburg, Germany, 27
John Donat Photography, London, England, 121, 141, 306, 348
Giorgio Dugnani for Domus, 113
Augustin Dumage, Paris, France, 116
Charles Eames, 327
John Ebstel, Philadelphia, Pa., 193-95
Gilles Ehrmann, Paris, France, 22
Bill Engdahl for Hedrich-Blessing, Chicago, Ill., 109
A. Fethulla Studio, Hiki, Finland, 270
Lionel Freedman, New York, N.Y., 335
Joshua Freiwald, San Francisco, Calif., 317, 318, 320
F/Stop Photo, San Francisco, Calif., 319
Alexandre Georges, Pomona, N.Y., 21, 178, 179, 182
German Information Center, New York, N.Y., 54, 65
Keith Gibson, Keighley, England, 308
Photo Gramma, 221, 330
Ken Grant, Santa Barbara, Calif., 138
Julien Graux, Paris, France, 60
Greater London Council, 4, 6
Russell Hamilton, 112
Hedrich-Blessing, Chicago, Ill., 107, 135, 191, 223, 254, 322
Heinrich Helfenstein, Zurich, Switzerland, 329, 344
David Hirsch, Brooklyn, N.Y., 283
Richard Hixson Photography, 316
Ilse Hofman, Briarwood, L.I., N.Y., 235
Hubert Hohn, 26
George Holton, 300
Yashuchiro Ishimoto, Kyoto, Japan, 248
© The Japan Architect, Tokyo, Japan: Masao Arai, 114, 149, 186, 232, 272, 285, 303, 350. Mitsuo Matsuoka, 31, 217, 276, 278. Taisuke Ogawa, 275, 333. Other, 229
J. Stewart Johnson, New York, N.Y., 102
Tore Johnson, Stockholm, Sweden, 247
Kawasaki, Tokyo, Japan, 174
Balthazar Korab, Troy, Mich., 12, 82, 92, 100, 125, 163, 165, 190, 239, 241, 336
Federico Kraft, 180
Sam Lambert, London, England, 3, 291, 302, 304
Peter Lanken, Montreal, Canada, 296
Lautman Photography, Washington, D.C., 262
Lehtilawa Oy, Helsinki, Finland, 81
Libbey-Owens-Ford Company, Toledo, Ohio, 151, 156
Nathaniel Lieberman, New York, N.Y., 25, 343
Michael Lyon, Austin, Tex., 75
William Maris, New York, N.Y., 42, 293
Barbara Martin, St. Louis, Mo., 128, 184
Laurin McCracken, 50
Norman McGrath, New York, N.Y., 24, 47, 167, 347
Joseph W. Molitor, Ossining, N.Y., 1, 88, 137, 201, 202, 216
Kaneaki Monma, Tokyo, Japan, 245
Ugo Mulas, 339
Osamu Murai, Tokyo, Japan, 10, 115, 132, 219, 287

Back cover: Sakakura Associates (Nishizawa,
Sakata, Nunokawa). Gumma Royal Hotel, Mae-
bashi, Japan. 1972-75. Photo: Photography
Dept., *Japan Architect*

Black flap: Gottfried Böhm. Housing, Cologne-
Chorweiler, Germany. 1969-75. Photo: Inge &
Arved von der Ropp

Inside back cover: Left: Emile Aillaud. Housing, Nanterre, France. 1969-78.

Right: Edgardo Giménez; mural by Uriburu.
Jorge Romero Brest House, Buenos Aires,
Argentina. 1971-73. Photo: Humberto Rivas